AQUA

THE KITCHEN

By Emelia Schiavetta

"I have written this book as an expression of gratitude to my family, past and present. A family so culturally diverse, whose zeal, warmth and teachings have coloured my life."

Emelia Schiavetta

Contents

Contents

Introduction

The first Aqua restaurant opened in 1998 on the waterfront of Bristol's Welshback, and four more have opened since. Aqua: The Kitchen holds a mirror up to all the Aqua restaurants and reflects the changing menus and culinary influences of the past sixteen years. During those years I have been asked countless times by customers for the recipes of our dishes, so they could reproduce them in their own kitchens… and so, here they are. Aqua: The Kitchen is an eclectic mix of those popular recipes and some of my own family secrets.

My father's family came to Scotland from Borgotaro, Italy, shortly after the war, moving from there to settle in London's Marylebone.

In the 60s my father owned a fish and chip restaurant called 'The Laughing Halibut' in London's Strutton ground, in Victoria. He also owned the Wimpy bar, the news agents and the betting shop!

It was there amongst the dense, claggy mists which rose from the fryers and permeated your skin, that I was born. It wasn't until I was thankfully packed off to school did the pungent effect finally fade.

My mother was born in India, of Dutch-Greek decent. She was a classically trained chef, if a rather reluctant one. To her relief, she noticed my passion for cooking, and it was under her eager instruction that I was taught the basic fundaments of French cookery. After I turned sixteen, she was rarely seen in the kitchen.

My most vivid memories as a small child were the summers spent with my Italian family, nona Emelia and aunt Emma. Their apartment was always full of people and food. Little attention was paid to decoration - all their focus and energy was reserved for food preparation and its eventual consumption.

There were food items in every corner. Dough rising in airing cupboards, the seductive vapours pacifying the soul;

freshly made pasta at varying stages of drying, suspended from ingeniously strung racks above our heads; and the hobs were alive with bubbling broths and sauces.

This was where my fascination for food began. I would spend my days learning pasta-making techniques and how to prepare sauce bases. Evenings at the dinner table were always lavish, lengthy and very colourful occasions. They left me with a sense of great appreciation and attention to detail, which I have carried with me in my own cooking. It is that enthusiasm that led me to write this book.

At school, I did well in art and domestic science, and after taking my O Levels, I went to the City of London College in Hoxton to study art. My love for design still remains, but as my father tirelessly reminded me, it would be my culinary skills that would pay the bills.

After much deliberation, I followed my father's advice, and took a HCIMA qualification at London's Westminster College. To be honest, this meant fleeting guest appearances, simply to pick up that week's work before disappearing to do something much more interesting! Somehow I managed to pass in the top five, and began work training in the kitchens of London's Grosvenor House Hotel, then finally in front of house.

Many restaurant and hotel kitchens later, I moved into private catering – cooking for those more blessed with wealth than me in London's Belgravia.

When I applied for a position as General Manager in a private members' club in Kensington, it was my future husband who interviewed me. I was successful, and just two years' later, Richard and I developed Aqua – the rest, as they say, is history.

Emelia Schiavetta

Antipasti

Piatto Acquatico

Just some small notes on this dish. You can use whatever fish skin you like for this recipe; bream, bass, trout the list is endless. I have used salmon skins as I like them to look as elongated as possible. I buy them from 'thefishsociety.co.uk' pre-prepped and descaled. Rather than a plain flour dusting, mix with cayenne pepper, fresh chilli, maize or herbs, etc. All can be adapted to this recipe, as long as the additions are dry.

The salt cod (or baccala) in this recipe is not exclusively Italian. Its origin could be staunchly challenged by the Spanish or the Portuguese. Nevertheless, I'm sure they would all agree that regardless whose claim to fame it actually is, it's divine.

I make the creamed baccala the day before it is served, as I like all the flavours to infuse overnight. The grissini I bake on the day, fresh and warm from the oven.

Serves   4 - 6

Shallow fried fish skins

For the fish skins:

6 salmon fillet skins, prepared by stockist

2 tbsp sea salt flakes

½ tsp smoked pimento powder

500ml peanut oil

1 heaped tbsp plain flour

Freshly ground black pepper

For the sweet & sour dipping sauce:

1 heaped tbsp soft brown sugar, dissolved in 5 tbsp of hot water

4 tbsp fresh lime juice

3 birds eye red chillies, deseeded and very finely sliced

4 tbsp fish sauce

1 tbsp of fresh chopped coriander

1 spring onion, topped & tailed, discarding 1 inch from the whitest end, then very finely sliced

1 large garlic clove very finely sliced

Method:

1. In a clean jar, with a tight fitting lid, mix all the dressing ingredients together, lid the jar, shake gently and place in the fridge for four hours or more before use.

2. Place the fish skins on a large plate, sprinkle with three quarters of the salt and leave for 40 minutes to tenderise.

3. After which time, rinse the skins well, pat dry with kitchen paper and lay them flat on a chopping board.

4. Heat the oil in a large skillet. When it reaches 190°C/375°F. Dust the skins with the remaining salt flakes, flour and pimento powder, season with black pepper and place the skins directly into the hot oil, using a large fish slice to keep the skins flat. Fry until crisp and golden. Drain on kitchen paper.

Creamed salt cod

For the creamed salt cod:

680g salt cod

1 large King Edward potato

1 medium white onion, finely chopped

2 large garlic cloves, crushed

100ml extra virgin olive oil

500ml whipping cream

Sea salt flakes and freshly ground black pepper

Pinch fresh nutmeg

For the grissini:

200g '00' Italian flour

100g potato flour

2 tsp instant dried yeast

1 tsp fine salt

75g unsalted butter

150ml whole milk, warmed

50g dolcelatte cheese

2 tbsp sesame seeds, toasted

1 egg, beaten

Sea salt flakes

Chef's tip:

You could try adding some finely chopped capers with mini gherkins to the creamed cod. Just make sure they are well drained.

Method:

1. Soak the salt cod in enough cold water to cover the fish. Leave overnight or for 48 hours if possible, changing the water often to remove excess salt.

2. Once soaked, rinse the fish thoroughly under cold water and pat dry.

3. Pre-heat the oven to 200°C/Gas 6 and bake the potato for 1 hour and 10 minutes.

4. Place the cod in a deep-sided pan with enough cold water to cover, plus two centimetres. Bring the water to a gentle simmer and cook for 20 minutes. Do not allow the fish to crumble.

5. Remove the cod and allow to cool, reserving a little of the poaching water.

6. Gently sauté the chopped onion in a little olive oil until translucent. Allow to cool. Once cooked, halve the baked potato and scoop out the flesh ready to use.

7. Flake the cod into a food processor with the blade attachment, discarding any skin or fine bones that may be present. Pulse lightly to break up the flesh. Add the crushed garlic and sautéed onions and pulse again. Then add the cream and potato flesh and run on a medium speed adding the olive oil in a thin stream. If after all the oil has been absorbed the mixture looks dense add a little of the poaching water to loosen.

8. Remove to a bowl, season well and add the nutmeg. Cover with cling film and refrigerate.

For the grissini:

1. Assemble a food mixer with the cake mix attachment, (or you can of course do this by hand), and add both flours and the salt to the mixer's bowl, away from the stand. Warm two tablespoons of the milk and mix with the yeast; let this stand while you rub the butter into the flours. Make a well in the centre of the mixture and add the yeast mix, drawing the flour mix in until completely combined.

2. In a separate bowl, break the cheese into small pieces and whisk with the remaining milk until smooth.

3. If using, put the mixer bowl back on the stand and add the cheese mixture to the dough. Run the mixer until you have a soft, sticky dough. Alternatively, if not using a mixer, stir the cheese mixture into the dough and knead in the bowl for five minutes. Cover the bowl with a damp cloth and leave for one hour.

4. Turn out the dough onto a lightly floured surface and knead for about two minutes, then cover with a damp towel and leave for a further hour.

5. Pre-heat the oven to 160°C/Gas 3 and line two baking trays with parchment.

6. This time, turn the dough out onto a clean work surface, using a small amount of flour if necessary. Roll the dough into a rectangle, 1cm thick. Cut into 25–30 strips and roll each strip into sticks using your hands. Place onto the baking trays and brush with the beaten egg, sprinkle with sesame seeds and salt flakes and bake for 35–40 minutes until golden brown. Serve the grissini warm with the creamed baccala.

Quail's egg wrapped in marinated anchovies

Ingredients:

8 medium boiled and peeled quail's eggs *(you can buy these already done at the supermarket)*.

8 fresh anchovy fillets preserved in oil

½ garlic clove, crushed

1 crushed pink peppercorn

½ tsp finely chopped flat leaf parsley

2 tbsp best quality olive oil

8 cocktail sticks

Method:

1. Place the olive oil, garlic, peppercorn and parsley in a small bowl and whisk together. Add the anchovy fillets to the oil mix and leave to marinate for one hour.

2. Once marinated, take one of the quail eggs, wrap an anchovy around the middle and secure with a cocktail stick. Continue to do this until all the eggs are wrapped.

Fresh oysters with Italian salami and a chilli saffron dressing

Ingredients:

8 fresh oysters, shucked, left in their shells

100g finely chopped Italian salami, peppery & smoky, such as 'sopressarta volpi'

For the chilli and saffron vinaigrette:

30ml white wine vinegar

5 tbsp extra virgin olive oil

1 heaped teaspoon of saffron threads

1 red birds eye chilli, deseeded and very finely sliced

Method:

1. Place the vinegar and saffron threads in a small saucepan and bring to the boil on a medium heat. As soon as it begins to boil, remove from the heat and let it stand for a good three hours to infuse. Once infused, add the olive oil, chilli and stir.

2. Gently fry the salami pieces in a small frying pan without oil, until lightly crisp, remove from the heat.

3. If your oysters are unshucked, begin to gently ease the oyster's flesh free from its connective tissue, with a small, sharp knife. Leave the oyster in its shell, and tip away any water residue.

4. Arrange the oysters on the plate of choice and begin to divide the salami pieces evenly on top. Lastly, spoon a teaspoon of vinaigrette over each oyster.

Melting mozzarella sticks with an arrabbiata dipping sauce

I first came across these gems in New York's little Italy. We were looking for a pre-dinner drink and fell upon a funky bar with great cocktails. With our drinks came these delights. They are incredibly easy and versatile, you can make up your own versions according to taste, as long as whatever you use to flavour them isn't wet or oily because that will make them soggy. If you stick to the consistency of a thick jam, you should be fine. If you're unable to find mozzarella sticks (I found them on Amazon), use small buffalo mozzarella balls, with the excess water pressed out, three in a line will make up a stick. Or grated cooking mozzarella is fine.

Serves   6   (3 each)

For the arrabbiata dipping sauce:

2 tbsp extra virgin olive oil

25g butter

1 onion, very finely chopped

3 large garlic cloves, crushed

3 small red chillies, deseeded and very finely chopped

1 tbsp tomato puree

2 x 400g cans cherry tomatoes

2 tbsp balsamic vinegar

40g flat-leaf parsley, chopped

Sea salt and freshly ground black pepper

For the mozzarella sticks:

18 extra-large spring roll wrappers, or large wontons, at room temperature

18 large mozzarella sticks or 54 small balls

600ml olive oil

Milk for brushing

1 dsp thick, homemade pesto

1 dsp onion marmalade

150g crisp cooked pancetta

1 chilli deseeded and very finely chopped

½ garlic clove crushed

7 black olives, stoned and finely minced

4 sun-kissed tomatoes, well drained

12 large fresh basil leaves

Method:

For the sauce:

1 . Heat a large frying pan over a medium heat. Add the butter and oil and fry the onion and garlic until very soft.

2 . Add the tomato puree and chopped chillies and cook for a further minute. Add the tinned tomatoes and gently simmer for about 15 minutes, until it thickens.

3 . Stir in the vinegar and parsley, cook for another minute, season well and remove from the heat to cool.

For the sticks:

1 . Divide the fillings into onion marmalade, pancetta and fresh basil; sun-kissed tomato and pesto; and black olive with chilli and garlic. Each set of ingredients will make six sticks. One at a time, lay the wraps on a damp tea towel. Spread the ingredients evenly across the wraps, leaving an inch border and lay the mozzarella sticks diagonally in the centre of the wraps to create a diamond shape.

2 . Take the bottom corner and fold it over the cheese, tucking firmly, then fold the left and right corners into the centre, firmly wrapping and completely covering the cheese. Brush the remaining border edges with milk and roll the wrap up, making sure it is well sealed. Continue to do this until you have filled all your wraps.

3 . Heat the oil in a deep, heavy-bottomed frying pan until quite hot. Fry the sticks, four at a time, until golden brown. Serve hot with the arrabbiata sauce.

Chef's tip:

These can also be baked in the oven. Preheat to 210°C/Gas 6, brush with a little olive oil and bake for 10–12 minutes, turning twice, until golden brown.

Toasted ravioli with sweet pepper dip

I use shop-bought ravioli for this recipe unless I have some dough leftover from a fresh batch I've made. Pre-prepared pasta is fine for this because you will be frying them, or you could bake them – it's up to you. Choose any filling you like, as long as it contains ricotta or some sort of cheese, so they have a good melting quality.

Serves 6

For the ravioli:

280g Panko breadcrumbs

450g Barts seasoned coarse breadcrumbs, or equivalent

170g Parmesan, grated

½ tsp flat-leaf parsley, finely chopped

½ tsp fresh oregano, finely chopped

24–28 fresh, cheese-filled ravioli

3 medium eggs

100ml whole milk

Sea salt flakes and freshly ground black pepper

400ml groundnut oil for frying

For the sweet pepper dip:

3 sweet red peppers, cored, deseeded, but left whole

3 plum tomatoes, deseeded, with cores removed and finely chopped

1 medium onion, finely chopped

1 small red chilli, deseeded and finely sliced

55g fresh basil, very finely chopped

2 garlic cloves, crushed

100ml extra virgin olive oil plus 3 tbsp for frying

2 tbsp balsamic vinegar

Sea salt flakes and freshly ground black pepper

Method:

1. Pre-heat the oven to 230°C/Gas 7. Line a baking sheet with parchment paper.

2. Place the peppers on a baking sheet, brush with olive oil and bake for 15 – 20 minutes, until the skins are lightly browned. Remove from the oven and place in a plastic bag to cool.

3. Meanwhile, in a medium frying pan, add three tablespoons of olive oil and fry the onions and garlic over a medium heat until soft, then add the vinegar, chopped tomatoes and chilli and fry for three minutes.

4. Peel the peppers, chop into chunks and place into a food blender, add the onion and tomato mix, place the lid on but remove the small central feeding top. Whizz on a medium setting while pouring in the remaining 100ml olive oil slowly through the feeding hole until smooth.

5. Transfer the dip to a bowl, add the chopped basil and season well. Cover with cling film and set aside.

6. If baking, line another baking sheet with parchment paper and turn the oven down to 200°C/Gas 6. If frying, you will just need a wire rack.

7. Get your bread crumbing station ready. Mix the eggs and milk in a low-sided bowl and season with salt and pepper. Place the Panko breadcrumbs on one plate and on a separate plate, mix the seasoned breadcrumbs, Parmesan and herbs.

8. One at a time, dip the ravioli in the egg mix, then into the Panko crumbs. Repeat the process of dipping into the egg, but this time press into the Parmesan seasoned crumbs.

9. If frying, place the coated ravioli on a plate while you wait for the oil to reach the required temperature. In a large skillet or wok, heat the groundnut oil until hot, drop a little pinch of the breadcrumbs into the oil, if they start to fizz, the oil is hot enough to fry the ravioli. If baking, place on the baking sheet and into the oven for about 10 – 15 minutes until a golden brown.

10. If frying, fry the ravioli in batches for approximately two minutes each side until golden brown. Drain on a wire rack.

11. Serve warm with the sweet pepper dip.

Small plate of savouries

As much as I love olives and cheese straws, sometimes I like to serve something a little more alternative for pre-dinner drinks. Although a bowl of nuts and some raw vegetables doesn't evoke much excitement, if you use the best quality ingredients you can source and spend the time to freshly grind your spices, you will notice the difference. Their taste and aroma are far superior to the pre-ground variety.

The raw butternut squash idea came from a friend, who had been for a meal at a local restaurant in Bellagio, Lake Como. She raved about this pre-dinner dish, and in fact, hardly mentioned the main event, just the squash! So I quizzed her endlessly on every element about the recipe that she could remember so I could replicate it... This is the outcome.

See overleaf for the recipe

Small plate of savouries

Serves   6

Pickled butternut squash

Ingredients:

1 dsp soft brown sugar

½ tsp sea salt flakes

100ml best quality extra virgin olive oil

1 crushed garlic clove

1 red chilli, deseeded and very finely sliced

1 ½ tsp fresh lemon thyme leaves

1 tbsp sherry vinegar

3 schezuan peppercorns, crushed

½ a medium butternut squash, peeled & seeded

1 tbsp pine nuts

Method:

1. Place all the ingredients except the squash and pine nuts in a large mixing bowl and whisk together to make the marinade, then set aside.

2. Cut the butternut squash into quarters, set up a food processor with the finest slicing blade or use a mandolin to slice the squash as thinly as possible.

3. Add the squash slices to the marinade and leave to stand for an hour or so.

4. Before serving, toast the pine nuts in the oven set at 200°C/Gas 5 and distribute over the squash salad.

Spiced nuts

Ingredients:

300g Marcona almonds *(borrowed from our Spanish friends for their excellent quality)*

1 egg white

1 clove

2 inch cinnamon stick

¼ tsp freshly ground nutmeg

The seeds from 1 cardamom pod

1 tbsp soft brown sugar

Method:

1. Pre-heat the oven to 190°C/Gas 5.

2. Line a baking sheet with parchment paper. Spread the nuts onto the baking tray and bake in the oven for five minutes or so, until they are beginning to brown. Remove them from the oven and allow to cool.

3. Place the spices in a spice grinder or equivalent and pulse to grind. Transfer to a small frying pan and lightly fry to release their aroma, then remove from the heat.

4. In a medium bowl, whisk the egg white until foaming.

5. Tip the nuts into the egg white and toss around, then add the spices to the bowl and toss again for an even coating.

6. Spread the nuts over the baking tray and bake for another five minutes, then sprinkle over the sugar and bake for a further three minutes. Allow to cool a little before serving.

Primi Piatti

Apple, speck and dolcelatte salad with a toasted hazelnut and raspberry dressing

Italian speck ham comes from the most northern province of Italy, Alto Adige. Although it boasts a delicate, smoked flavour, it's slightly more robust than hams such as Parma.

Serves   8

For the salad:

40g whole pistachio nuts, shelled

80g whole hazelnuts, shelled

4 Pink Lady apples

32 slices Italian speck ham *(from the Alto Adige region, if possible)*

Juice of ½ lemon

160g washed baby spinach

250g dolcelatte cheese

For the dressing:

125ml extra virgin olive oil

75ml hazelnut oil

1 tsp Dijon mustard

1 small bunch chives, very finely chopped

2½ tbsp raspberry vinegar

Sea salt and freshly ground pepper

Method:

1. Preheat the oven to 200°C/Gas 5.

2. Place all the dressing ingredients in a jar with a tight-fitting lid, season and shake well. Set aside.

3. Spread the hazelnuts on a roasting tray and bake until lightly golden. Remove from the oven and rub vigorously with a tea towel to remove the husks. Sprinkle with some salt and set aside.

4. Peel and core the apples. Slice them each into quarters, then quarter again. Squeeze the lemon juice over them and set aside on a plate.

5. Roughly crush the hazelnuts. Place in a large mixing bowl, add the spinach leaves, ¾ of the dressing and the apple slices. Lightly turn the salad with your hands to ensure evenly coated.

6. Place a handful of the salad onto cold serving plates, making sure each serving has four apple slices. Loosely roll each piece of speck into a rose shape and place four roses on each plate. Distribute the dolcelatte evenly onto each plate in small clumps, roughly half a teaspoon in size.

7. Lightly crush the pistachio nuts, sprinkle over each salad and spoon over the remaining dressing.

Chargrilled baby calamari with lime and garlic butter

Calamari (or squid) is a Mediterranean classic. I have chosen baby calamari for this recipe because they are more tender and quick to cook. The lime and garlic cuts through their sweetness for balance.

Serves   8

Ingredients:

2kg fresh baby calamari *(preferably cleaned)*

200g butter

Juice of 5 large limes

8 lime wedges

150ml extra virgin olive oil

6 garlic cloves, peeled

4 tbsp flat leaf parsley, finely chopped

Sea salt flakes and freshly ground black pepper

Method:

1. Blanch the garlic (I advise blanching garlic to remove any bitterness). To do this, place all 6 garlic cloves in a small pan of boiling water. Boil for two minutes then fish the cloves out with a small sieve and plunge into iced water. Repeat the process twice more, then crush the garlic and set aside.

2. Heat the butter on a medium heat in a large, heavy skillet. When the butter begins to bubble around the edges, add the lime juice and season well with salt and pepper. Add the pressed garlic and cook for one minute without browning. Stir in the parsley and remove from the heat.

3. Clean the calamari by pulling the tentacles away from the body, then remove the small translucent bone from the body's cavity. Discard the bone. Rinse the body well under cold running water. Holding the tentacles firmly with one hand, squeeze out the little beak, cut it away and discard, leaving the tentacles whole. Remove any guts or ink sacks. Rinse well under cold running water. Alternatively, ask your fishmonger to do this. If the calamari bodies are smaller than an inch in diameter, leave them whole, otherwise cut them so they are one inch thick. Pat dry with kitchen paper.

4. Heat a griddle pan until very hot, that is, just smoking. Lightly toss the calamari in approximately 60ml of the olive oil, then scatter half the calamari and tentacles in a single layer on the griddle (this will have to be done in a couple of batches). Cook the calamari at the highest heat possible without combustion! When the calamari blackens slightly on the underside, turn them over and do the same on the other side. Be careful not to char them too much as they will become bitter. When each batch is done, transfer to the lime butter pan and toss them around.

5. Serve with fresh crusty bread and lime wedges.

Caramelised endives with a warm Gorgonzola dressing and lamb's leaves

Bitter endives and creamy Gorgonzola work in harmony together in this dish. Belgian endives are known as 'white gold' and their pale green leaves are crisp and tangy.

Serves 8

For the caramelised endive:

8 Belgian endives

500g lamb's lettuce

1.5 litres chicken stock

Zest of 2 oranges cut into strands, plus their juices, divided

5 tbsp plain flour

25ml plus 75ml of lemon juice, divided

2 bay leaves

Zest of 1 lemon

½ tsp sea salt flakes

Freshly ground black pepper

250ml whole milk

4 tbsp soft light brown sugar, plus a little for blanching

150g butter plus 50g, divided *(alternatively use shop bought clarified butter)*

600g lamb's leaves

For the Gorgonzola dressing:

120g of good quality Gorgonzola cheese

6 tbsp homemade mayonnaise *(see page 167)*

Method:

1. Place the Gorgonzola over a bain marie *(see page 164)* and gently melt. Once melted, remove the bowl and add six tablespoons of homemade mayonnaise. Combine well, season and set aside.

2. Blanch the orange zest for 30 seconds in a small pan of boiling water with a teaspoon of soft brown sugar. Remove the zest and plunge into iced water. Repeat the process once more then drain and set aside.

3. Squeeze the orange juice into the same pan used for blanching. Add 25ml of lemon juice and boil until reduced to about four tablespoons of liquid. Set aside.

4. Put the endives, chicken stock, bay leaves, 75ml lemon juice and the zest into a deep sauté pan (with lid). Sprinkle half a teaspoon of salt over the mix and bring to the boil before turning down to a simmer. Cook for about 10 minutes or until a knife can be pushed through the endives easily. Place the endives tip end down in a colander to drain and allow to cool completely. Discard the liquid.

5. Press the cooled endives between some kitchen paper to remove any excess liquid (they need to be as dry as possible to caramelise). Cut the endives in half lengthways.

6. Mix the flour and sugar on a wide plate. Firmly roll the endives in the mixture until fully coated. Set aside until ready to sauté.

7. Clarify 150g of the butter by gently heating it in a small saucepan until melted - do not overheat. It should be possible to see the milk solids at the bottom when you tip the pan. Gently spoon the clarified butter into a separate bowl, leaving the milk solids behind. Alternatively, use shop bought clarified butter.

8. Heat the deep sauté pan used earlier on a medium heat and add the clarified butter. When the butter is hot, add the endives four at a time and cook for three minutes on each side until deep golden and very crispy. Set aside. Add the orange and lemon juice reduction to the same pan along with the orange strands. Heat lightly and spoon over the endive.

9. Place the lamb's lettuce in a mixing bowl. Run a little extra virgin olive oil over the leaves and lightly toss. Place a handful of lamb's leaves on each plate with two endive halves and drizzle with the Gorgonzola dressing.

Crab and prawn ravioli with shellfish sauce

This rich starter is so luxurious you only need a small amount per person. The recipe is slightly more complex than others, but worth it for a special dinner party.

Serves 6 (makes 24 raviolis)

For the ravioli filling:

400g raw white crab meat

200g raw peeled tiger prawns

1 dsp fresh finely chopped basil

1 dsp finely grated fresh ginger

1 dsp finely chopped fresh chervil

1 egg yolk

Juice of ½ a lemon

½ tsp ground white pepper

Sea salt & freshly ground black pepper

For the dough:

565g freshly made pasta (*see page 166*)

A little '00' flour for rolling, plus a little semolina flour for dusting

For the shellfish sauce:

1 litre shellfish stock (*see page 171*)

¼ tsp cayenne pepper

100ml double cream

Sea salt & freshly ground white pepper

Method:

1. Place the crab, prawns, herbs, ginger and egg yolk into a food processor and pulse until blended to a coarse breadcrumb texture. Decant the mix into a bowl; add the lemon juice and season to taste. Cover with cling film and refrigerate to firm up for one hour or however long it takes you to roll out your pasta!

2. Cut the pasta dough into quarters ready for rolling; ensure you keep the portions you are not rolling immediately wrapped up to stop them drying out.

3. Roll out each dough portion into one long sheet of pasta, then cut in half vertically so that once you have rolled out all the dough portions, you have eight sheets. Place two sheets at a time onto a lightly floured work surface or board and use a circular cutter to cut rounds out. I aim to get six circles per sheet.

4. Begin to make the raviolis by placing a heaped teaspoon of the crab mix in the centre of half the cut rounds, leaving a good half inch border around the edges for sealing.

5. Wet the edges with a little water or egg wash, then lay the remaining rounds on top, sealing them one by one. Begin to press the air away from the fillings' centre, then press down the edges firmly. Failure to be meticulous at this stage could mean that your raviolis will burst when cooked, due to trapped air. Repeat this process until all your raviolis are made. You may well end up with extra portions, which can be frozen.

6. Place the finished raviolis on a sheet of parchment paper with a little semolina flour dusted over it, to prevent sticking.

7. Bring a large pan of well-salted water to a boil for the pasta.

8. In a medium sized pan, bring the shellfish stock to a simmer. Reduce by ¼ then remove from the heat.

9. Drop the raviolis in the boiling water and cook for about six minutes, remember they will be al dente due to the semolina. Once cooked, remove to serving bowls.

10. Place the shellfish stock back on a low heat. Using an electric hand blender, begin to introduce the cream to the stock in a slow stream. Once heated through, add the cayenne pepper and seasoning. Remove the broth from the heat and turn the blender on high to produce a foaming broth.

11. Immediately ladle the broth over the ravioli and serve.

Crispy Thai fried soft shell crab with hot and sour dipping sauce

While soft shell crab is often seen in Asian cooking, they are still caught and cooked in Venice and considered a Venetian treat. Deep fried is the best way to enjoy them and with a contrasting sauce like this hot and sour dip.

Serves   8

Ingredients:

16 soft shell crabs, whole

400ml white wheat beer

30g fresh yeast

½ tsp caster sugar

½ tsp salt

2 tsp white balsamic vinegar

4 tsp finely chopped coriander

Juice of 2 limes

400g plain flour plus extra for dusting

1 litre peanut or sunflower oil

Sea salt flakes and freshly ground black pepper

Hot and sour dipping sauce *(see page 14)*

Method:

1. Prepare the hot and sour dipping sauce *(please refer to page 14)*.

2. Place the yeast, salt, pepper, vinegar, lime juice, coriander, sugar and beer in a large mixing bowl and whisk until smooth.

3. Sift the flour into the beer mixture and whisk until all lumps have disappeared. Set the batter aside to rest for one hour at room temperature.

4. Place some flour for dusting on a large plate and season. Place the peanut oil in a deep, sturdy wok or pre-heat a deep fat fryer to 190°C.   Test the temperature by dropping a cube of bread into the oil; it should sizzle immediately and turn brown if the oil is ready.

5. Cook the crabs two at a time, press the crabs into the plain seasoned flour then dip them in the batter, gently knock any excess batter off by slapping the crabs on each side of the bowl. Slide them into the oil to prevent any splashing. Fry for 3 – 4 minutes, turning until they are golden brown. Once cooked, transfer to a plate lined with two layers of kitchen towel to drain off any excess oil. Repeat the process until they are all cooked.

6. Serve the cooked crabs heaped in the middle of a plate with the hot and sour dipping sauce on the side.

Marinated black fig and glazed shallot salad with Parmesan and prosciutto crisps

Fresh black figs are an Italian staple. When Parmesan and prosciutto are added to the mix, you have a perfectly balanced sweet and salty combination.

Serves 8

For the salad:

8 fresh ripe black figs, halved

16 small shallots

170g fresh red chard

6 tbsp extra virgin olive oil

6 tbsp balsamic vinegar

1 tsp golden caster sugar

90g Parmesan cheese, freshly grated

16 thin slices of prosciutto

170g fresh watercress leaves

For the vinaigrette:

1 tsp Dijon mustard

1 garlic clove, very finely crushed

1 small red onion, very finely chopped

1 dsp runny honey

2 tbsp freshly squeezed lemon juice

200ml extra virgin olive oil

Sea salt flakes and freshly ground black pepper

Method:

1. Preheat the oven to 190°C/Gas 5.

2. Arrange the figs on a large flat dish so they fit easily without touching. Whisk together half the olive oil and balsamic vinegar and drizzle this over the figs, ensuring they are well coated. Cover with cling film and marinate in the fridge for 24 hours, turning a couple of times.

3. Whisk all the vinaigrette ingredients together, season well, then transfer to a jar with a lid and shake well. Set aside until needed.

4. Line two shallow baking trays with parchment paper. Shape the grated Parmesan into eight equal, flat, elongated triangles on each baking tray. Bake for 5–6 minutes until bubbling, but not browned. Remove from the oven and leave to cool on a wire rack until needed.

5. Using the baking trays you just used, lay the prosciutto slices on the lined baking tray, lay parchment paper over the prosciutto, then place the other baking tray on top to keep them flat, and cook for five minutes until crisp and lightly golden. Remove from the oven and place on kitchen towel until needed. Lower the oven temperature to 180°C/Gas 4.

6. Put the shallots on the baking tray and drizzle with the remaining oil and vinegar. Then sprinkle the caster sugar over the shallots and season well. Place the tray in the oven for 40 minutes. To prevent the shallots sticking, toss them gently every now and then, until nicely caramelised. Remove them from the oven and leave to cool. Once cooled, cut each shallot in half and set aside.

To assemble

Divide the watercress between eight plates, cut the figs into quarters, the shallots into halves and divide equally between the plates. Drizzle with the dressing and top with the Parmesan and prosciutto crisps.

Marinated mozzarella with preserved lemons and mint

This dish is a cross between Italian and Greek that works really well. The sharp, bitter lemons cut through the creamy mozzarella and the mint brings it all to life.

Serves   8

Ingredients:

8 fresh buffalo mozzarella, each loosely hand pulled apart

2 garlic cloves, very thinly sliced

40g preserved lemon rind

Juice of ½ a lemon

175ml extra virgin olive oil, plus 50ml extra

15 mint leaves *(make sure the mint leaves are young, not hard and coarse; if this means that they are very small then use more)*

200g pea shoots

Sea salt flakes and freshly ground black pepper

Method:

1. Place the mozzarella on a large flat dish. Scatter the garlic, preserved lemon rind and half the mint leaves over the cheese. Spoon over 175ml of olive oil, cover with cling film and refrigerate for at least one hour before serving (preferably longer).

2. Whisk together the 50ml of olive oil and the lemon juice and season well. Put the pea shoots in a large mixing bowl, add the oil and lemon dressing and turn the salad over a few times by hand.

3. Evenly distribute the pea shoots on the serving plates and place a portion of the marinated mozzarella on top and scatter the remaining mint leaves over. Serve with warm, crusty bread.

Mussels in a basil cream sauce

When people think of seafood, mussels are often ignored or avoided. They have adopted a dubious reputation for causing sickness if mishandled during preparation or cooking, which understandably is a bit of a put off.

Mussels you purchase these days are more often than not pre-sorted and need very little extra checking over. If you follow the basic rules of which molluscs to avoid, you will have no problems. The rules are; don't eat them if they stay open when raw, or stay closed when cooked.

Also, I visited Bruges recently and ate at a lovely little bistro, which I highly recommend, called Bistro de Pompe, kleine sint-Amandsstraat 2, Bruges 8000 Belgium, to my surprise mussels were not on the menu! When I enquired as to why the very gracious owner claimed he never sold mussels out of season, which is another good tip. The season for fresh mussels is from October to March.

Serves   8

Ingredients:

2kg fresh mussels, in their shells

150ml olive oil

2 medium onions, peeled and finely diced

2 celery sticks, trimmed, peeled and chopped

2 leeks *(white heads only)*, trimmed and chopped

4 garlic cloves, peeled and lightly crushed

800ml white wine

150ml double cream

Juice of ½ a lemon

250g fresh basil leaves

Sea salt flakes and freshly ground black pepper

Method:

1. To clean the mussels, put them in a basin of cold water with the cold water tap running over them. Scrape away any of the hard white matter with a knife. Remove any 'beards' (these are the hairy fronds that occasionally protrude from the outside of the the shell) by firmly pulling the beard down towards the narrow end of the shell. If any shells are slightly open, just tap them a couple of times against the side of the sink and press them shut. If they remain open, discard them. Rinse and set aside.

2. Add the olive oil to a deep saucepan large enough to accommodate the mussels, with a tight-fitting lid. Set the heat to medium; add the onion, celery, leeks and garlic. Stir well, then cover with the lid and sweat the mixture until soft, about 8−10 minutes. Remove the lid, add the wine, increase the heat and simmer until reduced by two thirds.

3. Now add the mussels to the stock pan, along with the strained stock, replace the lid and simmer for about 3−5 minutes, vigorously shaking the pan a couple of times until all of the shells have opened. Strain the mussels over a large bowl, reserving all the liquid, except the sandy, grainy residue at the bottom of the pan. Discard the sandy residue and any mussels that have failed to open. Put the mussels in a large bowl and squeeze the lemon juice over them. Cover with a damp tea towel.

4. Pour the reserved stock back into the pan and reduce a little. Remove from the heat, allow to cool a little, then slowly incorporate the cream using a hand blender to pulse the sauce for a minute or so. With the blender still running, add half the basil. Pulse for a further minute. Season to taste with the sea salt and black pepper and pour the sauce into a jug.

5. Return the mussels to the pan. Pour the sauce over the mussels and toss vigorously. On a low heat, warm this through slightly. Sprinkle the remaining basil leaves over and give the pot one, final toss.

6. Ladle into warm bowls and serve with warm, crusty bread.

Pan-seared scallops with garlic purée, crisp pancetta and basil oil

Scallops should be at their freshest when purchased, and at their freshest, they are also at their hardest to open, so save the cuts and scars and ask your fishmonger to open them for you.

Serves   6

Ingredients:

12 slices pancetta

24 queen scallops, shelled and cleaned with corals detached but retained

40g fresh basil

100ml extra virgin olive oil, plus extra for griddling

3 whole garlic bulbs, separated into cloves and peeled

200ml double cream

Sea salt and freshly ground black pepper

Dill for decoration

Method:

1. Blend the basil leaves with 100ml olive oil in a liquidiser and pulse for one minute. Pour the basil oil into a screw-top jar and set aside.

2. Pre-heat the oven to 190°C/Gas 5. Lay the pancetta slices on a parchment-lined baking tray, place another piece of parchment over the top and weigh down with another baking tray to keep the pancetta flat. Bake until crisp and dry, checking the pancetta after five minutes. Once crisp, cool on a wire rack and set aside.

3. Place the garlic cloves in a small pan of boiling water. Boil for two minutes then fish the cloves out with a small sieve and plunge into iced water. Then repeat the process twice more. Return the garlic cloves to the pan, add the cream and a pinch of salt, slowly bring to a simmer, stirring occasionally until the cream has thickened and the garlic is soft. Remove from the heat and allow to cool a little, then pulse the garlic cream in a liquidiser until smooth. Sieve the purée into a bowl and season to taste. Cover with cling film lightly pressed onto the surface to prevent skinning. Set aside.

4. Pat the scallops dry with kitchen towel. Heat a non-stick griddle pan over a medium to high heat. Brush the scallops and their corals with olive oil and season on both sides. When the griddle is very hot but not smoking, begin to sear the scallops and their corals. They must cook through, which will take roughly a minute to a minute and a half on both sides. Gently transfer the cooked scallops and corals to drain on kitchen towel.

5. Streak the basil oil over warm serving plates, dot or pipe four teaspoons of garlic purée on each plate. Arrange the scallops and corals as you wish. Break the pancetta into shards and lay them across the scallops.

Pigeon breast with pine nut, raisin and ricotta filled chocolate ravioli and a red wine jus

This recipe never fails to intrigue dinner guests each time we serve it. I first encountered this recipe in a small column of a Sunday Times magazine, and thought it was so interesting, so unexpected that I had to try it. Although originally designed as a main dish, I have adapted it and reduced it to a starter size. I believe people are willing to be adventurous with their starter but not their main. The addition of chocolate gives this dish wonderful depth, without being sweet. I'm aware it does appear to be an unusual combination but believe me, it works.

I suggest making the ravioli and stock a week ahead for any event and freezing them to reduce the workload. It is worth asking your butcher to fillet the pigeon breasts away from their carcasses, and be sure you keep the bones for the stock. Please note, I have given double the stock quantity needed as it makes a wonderful jus, (chef's gravy to us!), which I am in constant need of, as I'm sure are most households.

See overleaf for the recipe

Pigeon breast with pine nut, raisin and ricotta filled chocolate ravioli and a red wine jus

Serves 8 (makes 16 large ravioli)

For the pigeon breasts:

4 wood pigeons, breasts removed and carcasses kept for stock

1 star anise

1 large garlic clove, finely sliced

75cl good red wine

4 tsp extra virgin olive oil

100g butter, plus a little extra

For the stock:

850ml water

The pigeon carcasses

1 onion, peeled and chopped

2 shallots, peeled and chopped

2 large garlic cloves, finely sliced

1 carrot, peeled

1 celery stalk, trimmed

1 star anise

1 large bunch flat-leaf parsley

1 dsp redcurrant jelly

Sea salt and freshly ground black pepper

For the chocolate pasta dough:

340g '00' Italian pasta flour

60g good cocoa powder

4 medium eggs and 1 egg yolk, beaten

1 beaten egg, or a little whole milk, for brushing

3 tbsp cold water

For the ravioli filling:

80g plump, seedless raisins

250g ricotta cheese

100g pine nuts, toasted and cooled

Freshly grated nutmeg

Salt and pepper to taste

Small bunch chives, finely chopped

To decorate (optional):

25g salted butter

8 sage leaves

A little olive oil

A little plain flour

A little whole milk

Method:

For the marinade:

1. Marinate the pigeon breasts in half the red wine with the star anise and sliced garlic. Rest at room temperature for two hours, or if preparing a day in advance, refrigerate.

For the stock:

1. Chop the pigeon carcasses into a medium stockpot or large saucepan and begin to brown on a low heat with 1½ tablespoons of extra virgin olive oil and 25g butter. When browned, add the remainder of the wine, the water, vegetables, star anise and parsley. Bring to the boil, then simmer for 2½ hours without a lid to reduce the liquid by half, use this time to make the ravioli.

For the pasta dough:

1. Sift the cocoa powder with the pasta flour, and follow the instructions for basic pasta dough on page 166.

For the ricotta filling:

1. Blend the raisins and pine nuts in a food processor and pulse very lightly. Combine the ricotta, a good grating of nutmeg, chives and seasoning in a small bowl and add the raisin and pine nut mixture. Mix well, cover with cling film and place in the fridge.

2. Meanwhile, brush the sage leaves with milk, then dab each leaf in the flour. Heat the oil and butter in a medium frying pan until hot. Fry the sage leaves until crisp, drain on kitchen towel and set aside.

For the chocolate ravioli:

1. Roll out the sheets of pasta dough starting with the machine on the thickest setting, ending with it on the thinnest setting *(see page 166 for the best practice and techniques for rolling pasta sheets)*. Cut 32 pasta circles using an 8cm cookie cutter

2. Arrange half of the circles in rows and spoon a teaspoon of the filling into the centre of each, leaving a good 2cm edge to seal them well. Egg wash the edges, or brush them with milk and carefully place the remaining circles on top, forming the ravioli. It is essential that the covering discs are firmly pressed from the centre outwards before sealing them to remove any air trapped in the parcel. Then the edges must be sealed tightly. Set all finished raviolis aside on a piece of semolina dusted parchment paper to prevent sticking.

For the pigeon breasts:

1. Preheat the oven to 180°C/Gas 4.

2. In a large saucepan, bring well-salted water to the boil.

3. Strain the pigeon carcass stock through a fine sieve. Pour half the stock into another sturdy saucepan on a high heat and reduce by half until thick and glossy. Keep warm. Freeze the remaining stock to use another time.

4. Remove the pigeon breasts from the marinade and pat dry with kitchen towel. Heat an oven-proof frying pan on a medium to high heat with two tablespoons of oil and 50g butter. Fry the breasts for one minute on each side, until lightly browned, then put the pan in the oven for a further four minutes.

5. Remove the pan from the oven, place the breasts on a plate, cover with foil and allow to rest. Add the reduced stock to the frying pan used to cook the pigeon breasts and add the redcurrant jelly. Leave to bubble gently on a low heat.

6. Cook the ravioli in the boiling water for 5–7 minutes. Remove with a slotted spoon and drain on a damp tea towel.

7. Pour the red wine reduction through a sieve into a pouring jug. Slice each pigeon breast into three long strips so that they 'fan out'. Place a spoonful of the red wine reduction in the centre of each plate with one ravioli on top, drizzle a little more reduction over the ravioli. Fan the pigeon breast on top, then another ravioli, drizzle more reduction and decorate with the fried sage leaves and serve immediately.

Salt cod

Salt cod is widely used in Mediterranean kitchens. Contrary to expectations, given its name, the fish has a delicate, deep flavour which is not at all salty.

Once the cod has been soaked, all saltiness is removed and the cod can then be used in a wide variety of dishes.

Salt cod and prawn tortellini with a foaming leek sauce

Serves   8   (makes 48 large tortellini)

Please note the salt cod requires 24-36 hours pre-soaking

For the tortellini:

565g fresh pasta dough *(see page 166)*, rolled out into 8 sheets.

For the filling:

225g salt cod

2 garlic cloves, crushed

1 shallot, finely sliced

15 large raw prawns, peeled and cleaned

1 large potato, baked, flesh removed and skins discarded

180ml double cream

50ml olive oil for frying

Sea salt and freshly ground black pepper

¼ tsp white pepper

For the sauce:

500g baby leeks, washed and finely sliced

250ml chicken stock *(see page 170)*

300ml double cream

½ tsp mustard powder

40g butter

50ml olive oil

For the egg wash:

1 egg, beaten

Method:

1. In a large bowl or saucepan, cover the salt cod in cold water and leave to soak for 24 – 36 hours, changing the water every four hours.

2. Once the cod has been soaked, drain the water away and rinse the cod thoroughly. Bring a deep sauté pan of water to simmer. Place the cod in the simmering water and poach for 10 minutes. Turn the heat off and leave the cod in the poaching water for a further 15 minutes.

3. Remove the cod from the water with a slotted spoon, place on a plate and allow to cool. Once cooled, remove and discard any bones or skin present, then flake the cod and set aside.

4. Heat 25ml of olive oil in a frying pan and gently sauté the shallots and garlic until soft but not browned. Remove from the pan and set aside.

5. In the same pan, heat the remaining 25ml of oil and begin to fry the prawns until just pink. Do not brown them. Allow to cool and set aside.

6. Pour 180ml of cream into a small saucepan and bring to a light simmer then remove from the heat. Put the cod and prawns into a food processor bowl; add the shallots, garlic and half the warm cream and pulse into a smooth paste. Add the potato flesh and the remaining cream and pulse until smooth. Add a good pinch of salt and white pepper. Cover with cling film and refrigerate until needed.

7. Cut 48 circles of pasta using an 8cm circular cutter. Lay the circles on a clean, lightly floured surface. Put one good teaspoon of filling in the centre of each circle, leaving a good 2cm edge for sealing, then lightly brush the edges with egg wash and fold them over so they form a half-moon shape. Press out any trapped air when closing and sealing the tortellini. Pinch the edges down tightly to seal them. Bring the two ends of the semi-circular tortellini together by wrapping them around your index finger to make a cone and pinch their tips together tightly. Now roll the top of the cone down from your fingertip like a roll-neck sweater, and the tortellini are formed. Place them on parchment paper to prevent sticking as you go.

8. Bring a medium saucepan of salted water to boil and blanch the leeks for a couple of minutes. Refresh in cold water and drain, but retain the pan and the hot water.

9. Melt the butter and oil in a saucepan and lightly sweat the leeks for about eight minutes, without browning. Add the chicken stock, cream and mustard powder and simmer for a further five minutes. Then whizz using a hand blender until smooth. Pass the sauce through a sieve into a bowl, cover the bowl with a damp cloth to prevent skinning and set aside.

10. Bring the retained leek water to a gentle rolling boil.

11. Put the tortellini in the boiling water for 5 – 7 minutes to ensure they are cooked through. With a slotted spoon, transfer the cooked tortellini onto a clean, dry tea towel to drain.

12. Place three tortellini into warm serving bowls. Reheat the sauce lightly and ladle a little into each bowl around the tortellini. Froth the remaining sauce with a hand blender until foam-like and ladle over. Serve immediately.

Seared veal carpaccio with shallot confit and garlic vinaigrette

The Italians love veal and it has been making a comeback over here, thanks to the emergence of the more ethical rose veal. Make sure you buy the finest veal you can for this dish. Skimping on the quality does reflect on the finished dish.

Serves 6

For the carpaccio:

600g whole veal rump, in one piece, trimmed

1 large onion, peeled and roughly chopped

2 carrots, peeled and roughly chopped

20g unsalted butter

2 tbsp vegetable oil

5 sprigs thyme

Sea salt flakes and freshly ground pepper

For the shallot confit:

6 shallots, peeled and finely chopped

100ml extra virgin olive oil

For the vinaigrette:

200ml extra virgin olive oil

50ml balsamic vinegar

2 garlic cloves, peeled and crushed

1 sprig thyme

1 sprig rosemary

Sea salt flakes and ground black pepper

For the garnish:

120g lamb's lettuce

4 tbsp Parmesan shavings

Method:

1. For the vinaigrette, whisk the olive oil, balsamic vinegar and seasoning together in a bowl. Add the remaining ingredients and transfer to a screw-top jar. Leave to infuse for two hours.

2. Place the chopped shallots into a small saucepan and cover with 100ml of extra virgin olive oil. Cook slowly over a very low heat until translucent and very soft, which takes roughly 30 minutes. Set aside.

3. Preheat the oven to 230°C/Gas 8. Season the veal on all sides with salt and pepper and heat a large oven-proof frying pan over a high heat.

4. Add the vegetable oil, then the butter to the pan and once melted, sear the whole rump for two minutes on all sides until the meat has browned. Remove from the pan and set aside.

5. Add the chopped carrots, onions and the thyme sprigs to the same pan and cook for four minutes. Lay the veal on top of the vegetables and put the pan in the oven for six minutes. Remove from the oven and allow to rest in the pan until cold.

6. Sieve the vinaigrette and set aside. Then slice the rested veal as thinly as possible, across the grain. Mix five tablespoons of the vinaigrette with the shallot confit and spoon onto the serving plates, spreading it around the plate using the back of the spoon. Place the lamb's lettuce into a mixing bowl and toss lightly with a little of the remaining vinaigrette. Arrange the veal slices over the leaves, allowing about five slices per portion. Evenly spoon over the remaining confit and vinaigrette, top with Parmesan shavings.

Secondi Piatti

Aubergine parmigiana with a rocket and basil salad

This recipe was passed down to me by my grandmother Emelia. There are a few versions of this dish and claims to its correct assembly. The south claims it as their own, as does the northern province of Palma. The "correct" way to make this dish is still a dispute. To crumb or not to crumb!

The south typically would crumb the aubergine before frying or use a mixture of grated Parmesan and breadcrumbs as a topping. The north swings both ways and I am sticking to my nonna's recipe, which is without crumb, but please feel free to do as you wish.

Serves 6

You will need six 13cm–15cm individual, non-stick cooking rings, 8cm deep. Alternatively, you could use one large rectangular dish.

For the aubergine parmigiana:

5 medium aubergines

500g buffalo mozzarella, thinly sliced

150g finely grated fresh Parmesan cheese

60g fresh torn basil

Olive oil for frying

3 tbsp fine cooking salt

600g fresh pomodoro sauce *(see page 168)*

Plain flour for dusting

For the salad and dressing:

200g fresh rocket

200g fresh basil

2 tbsp extra virgin olive oil

1 tbsp fresh lemon juice

Sea salt and freshly ground black pepper

Method:

1. Pre-heat the oven to 190°C/Gas 5. Slice the aubergines into 5mm circles, arrange on a large platter and sprinkle cooking salt all over. Allow about 40 minutes for the bitter black juices to be released. Rinse the aubergine thoroughly under cold running water and pat dry with kitchen paper. Coat the aubergine with a little seasoned plain flour.

2. Heat a large frying pan with olive oil over a medium to high heat and fry the aubergine in batches until browned. Once browned, place on a plate double-lined with kitchen towel to soak up any oil residue and set aside.

3. Butter the cooking rings (or rectangular dish) well and place them on a non-stick baking sheet. Arrange a layer of aubergine at the bottom of each ring, and then place a dessertspoon of pomodoro sauce over and a good sprinkle of the basil. Add a layer of mozzarella , followed by Parmesan and repeat this process until there are three layers, ending with the mozzarella and Parmesan. Sprinkle with salt and pepper and bake in the oven for about 25 minutes until browned. Remove from the oven and leave to set for five minutes before serving

4. Meanwhile, beat the extra virgin olive oil and lemon juice together in a large bowl and season to taste. Place the rocket and basil in the bowl, and turn the ingredients together using your hands.

5. Use a large flat spatula to remove the rings from the baking sheet. Place each ring in the centre of a pre-warmed plate and run a sharp knife around the edge to release the aubergine. Shape a handful of the salad on top of each round and serve.

Secondi Piatti

Capelli d'angelo with crab chilli and samphire

This is the fastest dish to prepare in the book. It's fresh, healthy and very light. Capelli d'angelo pasta literarily translates to 'angel hair' as its strands are incredibly fine, enabling the delicate crab meat and samphire to shine through without the pasta dominating.

Serves 6

Ingredients:

350g white crab meat, flaked and separated

90ml extra virgin olive oil, plus 1 tbsp

3 cloves garlic, crushed

2 red chillies, deseeded and diced very finely

450g angel hair pasta

3 tbsp fresh basil, chopped

75 – 100ml dry white wine

4 spring onions, thinly chopped diagonally

Zest of 1 lime

250g samphire

Sea salt and freshly ground black pepper

Method:

1. Lightly steam the samphire for about two minutes, plunge into ice cold water, drain and set aside until needed. Bring a large pan of well-salted water to the boil and cook the pasta for three to four minutes. Refresh with cold running water and add one tablespoon of olive oil to separate each strand and prevent clagging.

2. Heat the olive oil in a large frying pan, add the spring onions, chilli and garlic and sauté for two minutes, adding some pepper but not salt (the samphire is salty enough).

3. Add the white wine and reduce for about a minute, then add the crab meat, lime zest, samphire and pasta. Tong the mixture thoroughly, heat and serve immediately.

Crisp-braised belly pork with a butter bean, chorizo and garlic ragu

It's important to stress that this cooking technique requires a long resting time; preferably in the fridge overnight. The ragu can be prepared at the same time and refrigerated until needed. This, obviously, has the advantage of enabling you to prepare and cook the main elements of the dish the day before you intend to serve it. I recommend using 'El Navarrico' butter beans - judion de la granja - because they are of the highest quality. Using these beans has the advantage of not having to soak and so on. I have tried soaking other raw butter beans but they are never as good. Nor are any tinned variety I've tried.

Serves   8

For the bean ragu:

2 x 425g jars 'El Navaricco' butter beans

500g spicy parrilla picante cooking chorizo

100ml olive oil

10 garlic cloves, finely sliced

1 onion, finely chopped

250ml white wine

2 cans chopped tomatoes

3 tbsp flat-leaf parsley

For the pork belly:

1.3kg pork belly, in one piece

2 bulbs garlic

175ml white wine

9 sprigs thyme

450ml chicken stock

Sea salt flakes and freshly ground black pepper

A little olive oil

Method:

1. Pre-heat the oven to 170°C/Gas 3.

2. Score the skin side of the pork belly with a very sharp knife, making cuts about half an inch apart. Turn the belly over and rub the flesh with salt and pepper and set aside.

3. Line a roasting tray large enough to accommodate the pork with double tin foil and then top the foil with a non-stick baking mat or equivalent. Besides stopping the foil from sticking to the pork, it also makes cleaning the tray a lot easier, as the pork will be in the oven for a long time.

4. Rub the outer husks of the garlic bulbs away and cut them horizontally, resulting in four halves, then place them on the non-stick baking mat and drizzle with olive oil. Scatter the thyme over the garlic and lay the pork belly on top, skin side up. Rub a little olive oil on the scored skin and rub in some sea salt flakes. Pour the white wine and chicken stock around the pork, cover the whole tray with tin foil and bake for 2½−3 hours until tender. Baste the pork a couple of times with the pan juices during cooking.

5. Once cooked, transfer the pork to a clean roasting pan, place a piece of baking parchment over the pork's skin, then place another baking tray on top of the meat and weigh it down with a heavy object (this compresses the pork and shapes it). Allow to cool. The pork must be left for several hours in the fridge, preferably overnight.

6. To make the ragu, drain and rinse the butter beans. Cut the chorizo into thin slices. Heat the olive oil in a deep sauté pan on a medium heat and add the garlic. When the garlic sizzles, add the chorizo and cook until lightly browned. Turn out onto a plate. Reduce the heat and lightly fry the onion in the same pan, until translucent. Return the garlic and chorizo to the pan, turn the heat back to medium and add the white wine. Reduce until the liquid has almost evaporated. Add the tomatoes and butter beans, salt, pepper and half the parsley and simmer for 15 minutes. Remove from the heat, cool, then refrigerate until needed. Scatter the remaining parsley over when ready to serve.

7. Pre-heat the oven to its highest temperature (250°C/Gas 9). Cut and trim the pressed pork into individual portions and pat dry with kitchen paper. Place the portions skin side down in a frying pan and seal for two minutes on a high heat. Now place the pork skin-side up on a baking tray lined with foil and parchment paper. Drizzle with olive oil and sprinkle with salt flakes. Roast the pork belly for about 15 minutes until the skin is crispy and brown. Heat the ragu through. Rest the pork for 5−7 minutes before serving on top of the heated ragu.

Done-to-death duck with yellow spiced rice

Done-to-death duck has to be one of the most popular dishes we have ever served in Aqua, no doubt because of its soft, juicy texture and rich flavours. 'DDD' as it's better known, periodically makes a guest appearance on the specials menu due to popular demand, and it is included here for nostalgia's sake as a truly retro Aqua dish. This dish does require lengthy preparation but it is an exceptional dish for a special occasion. You must allow 24 hours for the curing and a further 6 to 7 hours for the confit cooking and cooling process. You can confit the duck a week or more in advance, as long as the fat that the duck has cooled in is not disturbed in any way.

Allowing the duck to cool while completely immersed in fat ensures that the meat is protected from the air. The fat provides an impermeable barrier and is one of the oldest forms of preservation.

See overleaf for the recipe

Done-to-death duck with yellow spiced rice

Serves   8

For the confit:

8 duck breasts, trimmed, about 175g each, boned weight, skins intact

2 litres duck fat (melted) or vegetable oil

10 sprigs thyme

3 bay leaves

4 star anise

8 garlic cloves, peeled and roughly sliced

1 large white onion, sliced into rough rings

500g table salt

1 tsp ground white pepper

2 tsp onion salt

For the yellow spiced rice:

4 dsp groundnut oil

500g basmati rice

1½ dsp turmeric

1 cinnamon stick

1 star anise

1.2 litres vegetable stock *(stock pots or cubes are acceptable)*

2 garlic cloves

Sea salt and freshly ground pepper

For the stir-fried vegetables:

400g mixed, sliced sweet peppers (not green)

1 large red onion, peeled and thinly sliced

140g fine green beans, topped, tailed and sliced lengthways

100ml groundnut oil

For the teriyaki sauce:

200ml dark soy sauce

550ml water

1½ tsp fresh, minced ginger

1 tsp fresh, minced garlic

400g soft, dark-brown sugar

2 tbsp clear honey

4 dsp corn flour and a little water to make a paste

For the decoration:

1 heaped tsp of toasted sesame seeds

8 large wonton wrappers

1 litre groundnut oil for deep-frying

Method:

The curing – 24 hours:

1. Sprinkle 250g of salt over the bottom of a deep roasting tray. Put the bay leaves, thyme sprigs, onion salt, white pepper and star anise in a food processor with the remaining 250g of salt. Pulse the mixture for a minute or so, to produce a spiced salt.

2. Place the duck into the pan, rub half of the spiced salt into the duck skin thoroughly. Scatter the garlic over the duck. Then layer the white onion rings on top. Completely cover the meat with the remaining spiced salt mix, creating a thick crust.

3. Wrap the tray in cling film and cure in the fridge for 24 hours…

The baking – 3 hours:

1. … After which time, pre-heat the oven to 150°C/Gas 2. Gently dust the salt crust from the cured meat, rinse under cold water and pat dry with kitchen paper. Discard any remaining salt used for the curing from the roasting tray, and wipe the tray clean.

2. Place the duck in the tray and immerse in two litres of melted duck fat or vegetable oil, then bake in the oven for three hours.

3. Remove the duck from the oven and allow to cool in the fat/oil until completely cold. Do not be tempted to agitate or disturb the fat in any way.

The teriyaki sauce:

1. Place all the ingredients, except the corn flour, in a medium saucepan and begin to heat gently until the sugar has dissolved, then remove from the heat. In a small glass, dissolve the corn flour in enough water to make a paste and add this to the soy sauce mixture, mix thoroughly and return the pan to the hob. Increase the heat to reduce the liquid, continue to mix until the sauce begins to thicken. Let this simmer gently for 10 minutes. Pass the sauce through a sieve to remove any garlic and ginger sediment. Transfer to a small bowl and allow to cool, then cover with cling film and refrigerate.

The yellow spiced rice:

1. Use a medium to large saucepan with a tight-fitting lid. Crack the star anise with the back of a dessertspoon, crush the garlic cloves, snap the cinnamon stick in half and toss these ingredients into the saucepan with the turmeric and groundnut oil. Gently fry for two minutes whilst lightly stirring to release the flavours.

2. Add the rice to the spices and coat the grains thoroughly. Add a teaspoon of salt and a good grind of black pepper.

3. Pour the vegetable stock into the rice and bring to a light boil, then immediately turn the heat down to the lowest it will go and pop the lid on. Leave the rice to cook gently for 20 minutes. When all the liquid has evaporated and small holes appear on the surface, it's ready.

The stir-fried vegetables:

1. Heat the groundnut oil in a frying pan over a medium heat. Fry the sliced peppers and red onion slices until golden. Add the green beans and stir. Add two tablespoons of the teriyaki sauce to the pan and stir into the vegetables. Remove from the heat and set aside until needed.

The final cooking:

1. Pre-heat the oven to 200°C/Gas 6.

2. Heat the litre of groundnut oil in a deep fat fryer, large pan or wok to 175°C/350°F. Once the temperature is reached drop the wonton wrappers individually into the oil – they crisp up in seconds. Once cooked, leave to drain on kitchen towel.

3. Start to remove all the preservation fat from the duck and wipe away any residue with kitchen towel, leaving the skin intact.

4. Using a large, sturdy oven-proof frying pan, begin to brown the duck by laying it skin-side down in the pan on a medium heat (there is no need for any extra oil or fat to be added). Fry the duck breasts for 3–4 minutes without disturbing them. Then take a ladle of the teriyaki sauce and spoon it around the pan. Lift the duck joints to enable the sauce to coat the skin, as they will caramelise in the oven. Place the pan in the oven for 6–8 minutes to warm the duck through thoroughly.

5. When serving, heat through a ladle of the teriyaki sauce in a small pan, also heat through the vegetables.

6. Take the duck breasts out of the oven. Remove the lid from the rice and remove the star anise and cinnamon. Place a portion of the rice onto each serving plate, portion the vegetables, then place one duck breast, skin side up, on top of the vegetables. Spoon a couple of tablespoons of the heated teriyaki reduction over the duck, sprinkle over a few of the sesame seeds and place the wonton between the two like a sail. Serve immediately.

Duck pappardelle

Any robust meat is ideal for producing a ragu to stir through thick strips of pappardelle. We serve slow roasted duck with ours at the restaurant and it's been well received.

The word pappardelle derives from the verb 'pappare', which means to gobble up! And if the very clean plates we clear are anything to go by, I think you'll like it. You could prepare the duck the day before for ease.

Serves 4

Ingredients:

3 duck legs

4 tbsp olive oil

1 tsp Chinese five spice

2 rosemary sprigs, picked and stripped

1 tsp chopped parsley

3 oranges, plus 2 quarters

200g red onions

200g spring onions

125ml dry marsala wine

1 tsp chopped thyme

1 tsp chopped sage

240ml double cream

75ml sherry vinegar

100ml vegetable stock

500g dried Pappardelle pasta

Sea salt and freshly ground black pepper

Method:

1. Pre-heat the oven to 140°C/Gas 1.

2. Squeeze the juice of three oranges into a small roasting tray and add the vegetable stock. Rub the duck legs with the five spice and place them in the roasting pan. Sprinkle the rosemary over the duck and season well, cover the tray with a sheet of doubled tin foil, seal around the edges and slow roast for three hours.

3. After cooking, allow the legs to cool, then strip the meat from the bone in large shreds and set aside. Discard any fat or liquid left in the roasting pan and wipe the pan clean.

4. Turn the oven up to 200°C/Gas 6.

5. Cut each red onion into six segments and put them into the cleaned roasting pan. Pour two tablespoons of olive oil over the onions, season and roast for 20 minutes. Remove from the oven and allow to cool. Once cooled, remove any over-cooked leathery outer skin and set aside.

6. Bring a medium saucepan of well-salted water to the boil, add the pappardelle and cook for about 6−8 minutes. Strain the pasta and rinse with boiled water, then drizzle a little olive oil over the pasta to prevent it from sticking. Keep the pasta warm whilst making the sauce.

7. Heat the remaining olive oil in a deep frying pan, add the duck meat and red onions and fry for a minute. Add the spring onions, sage, thyme, juice from the orange quarters, the vinegar and marsala wine and cook for one minute on a high heat. Then add the double cream and cook for a further minute. Now add the pasta, parsley, salt and pepper and heat through for about two minutes, serving immediately.

Thai green monkfish and tiger prawn curry

Another very popular retro dish. We actually served this curry three ways, with monkfish, chicken breast or vegetarian, all of which worked well. If we've got a lot of people to feed on Boxing Day I've often used this dish, as it's so easy.

Serves   8

Ingredients:

1.2kg fresh monkfish fillets, boned and skinned

40 raw tiger prawns, peeled, tails on

155g Thai basil *(if you can't get Thai basil use normal basil)*

2 large green chillies or 4 small, deseeded *(keep the seeds)*

2 lime leaves

155g fresh coriander

3 x 400ml cans of coconut milk

10 garlic cloves

3 tbsp Thai fish sauce

700g fine green beans

1 tbsp fresh ginger, minced

1 tbsp palm sugar

3 fresh lemon grass, trimmed and cut into ½ inch slices

1 tsp shrimp paste

Method:

For the curry sauce:

1. Take a very large bowl (preferably one that can be accommodated in the fridge) and add all the ingredients, except for the monkfish, tiger prawns and green beans.

2. Pulse with an electric hand-blender until the sauce is smooth and lump free. Test the flavour with a teaspoon. If more chilli heat is required add a few of the seeds that were set aside. Blend and re-test until the curry sauce is to your taste. Cover the bowl with cling film and refrigerate for two hours, or preferably over night

3. After which time, take out the sauce to reach room temperature.

For the seafood:

1. Meanwhile, dry the monkfish off with kitchen towel and cut into two inch squares.

2. Heat the curry sauce in a pan on a medium heat. This would be a good time to start cooking your rice or noodles to serve it with.

3. When the sauce starts to form small bubbles around the edge of the pan, gently place the monkfish pieces into the sauce. Very lightly simmer for five minutes, without a lid.

4. Then drop the raw prawns in and gently stir them into the curry sauce. Leave for three minutes or so, before gently folding the seafood into the sauce. When all the prawns have turned pink it's ready, serve immediately.

Fusillo calabro with scallops and garlic

Fusillo calabro is a long, corkscrew shaped pasta. It has a thick density and is usually served with thick, hearty sauces and meats, or in this case, scallops. There are quite a few types of fusillo, short tight spirals, flat with a twist, and so on. I have used the long tubular type with a slight twist, which has an elegant appearance unlike the short spirals, which remind me of school dinners!

Serves   6

Ingredients:

500g dried fusillo calabro pasta

24 large king scallops, with coral on

2 garlic cloves, thinly sliced

100g butter

100ml olive oil

3 tbsp chopped flat leaf parsley

150ml dry white wine

Zest of 1 lemon

Freshly ground sea salt and pepper

Method:

1. Wipe the scallops clean with kitchen towel. Put the olive oil and sliced garlic in a bowl, add the scallops and marinate for an hour.

2. After the hour, put a large pan of well-salted water on to boil and heat a griddle pan until very hot.

3. Cook the fusillo in the boiling water for 10−12 minutes (fusillo calabro is quite thick and needs a little time).

4. Take the scallops out of the marinade, retaining the marinade and sear the scallops on the hot griddle. They need about one minute undisturbed on each side, although this really does depend on their size.

5. While the scallops are searing, heat 75g of butter in a large sauté pan with the retained marinade. Cook on a medium heat for a minute, keep stirring so the garlic doesn't colour (remember to turn the scallops over during this time.) Add the white wine and cook for a further minute, then add the parsley and lemon zest and remove from the heat without cooking further. Remove scallops from the griddle to the sauté pan.

6. Drain the pasta but keep a ladleful of the pasta water. Put the sauté pan back on the heat; then add the pasta, the small ladle of pasta water and the remaining butter and heat through. Season to taste and serve immediately.

Herb-crust rack of lamb with dauphinoise potatoes

This dish is unashamedly French for an Italian kitchen to produce, but I have defiantly decided to include it, as it is one of the favourites in the restaurants.

This is an essentially simple meal and as such it relies a great deal on the quality of the ingredients. Buy the meat from a highly reputable butcher (ask your butcher to French-trim the lamb rack). You need 3 – 4 chops on each rack, so consult the butcher about the best configuration of the racks – sometimes they come with eight chops, sometimes with six. The dauphinoise potatoes can be prepared a day in advance.

Serves   6

For the lamb:

6 x racks of lamb, French-trimmed, each with 3 – 4 chops, fat scored

40g unsalted butter

5 tbsp Dijon mustard

25ml olive oil

500ml red wine jus *(see page 167)*

150g stale, white bread, broken into small pieces

150g fresh flat-leaf parsley

150g fresh basil

150g fresh thyme

50g fresh chives

100ml extra virgin olive oil

Sea salt and freshly ground black pepper

For the dauphinoise potatoes:

1.25kg King Edward potatoes

700ml whipping cream

4 large, crushed garlic cloves

½ tsp white pepper

Sea salt flakes and freshly ground pepper

7 sprigs fresh thyme

1 level tsp fine cooking salt

Method:

1. Pre-heat the oven to 190°C/Gas 5. Peel the potatoes and run them through the thin-blade slicer of a food processor, so that the slices are wafer thin. When they are all sliced, tip them into a shallow 5 – 7cm deep baking tray and season them well with the salt and a few good grinds of black pepper. Strip the small leaves from the thyme stems and sprinkle the leaves, crushed garlic and white pepper over the potatoes. Rub these ingredients thoroughly through the potatoes by hand.

2. Pour the cream evenly over the potatoes and press down, so that the cream just covers them. Cover the tray with tin foil and place in the oven for one hour, then remove the foil and cook for a further hour until golden brown. Insert a knife into the centre to ensure they're cooked through. Set aside.

3. Place the stale bread in a food processor and pulse to a coarse crumb. Add the parsley, basil, thyme and chives, season the mixture and drizzle 25ml of olive oil through the feeding top and pulse to a fine consistency. The mixture will take on a lovely, verdant hue. The crumb mixture should be moist but not sticky. Spread the mixture onto a large plate and set aside until needed.

4. Pre-heat the oven to 220°C/Gas 7. If you have dauphinoise potatoes pre-prepared, then now is the time to re-heat them for 15 – 20 minutes.

5. Heat the oil and butter in a large, oven-proof frying pan until hot. Season each lamb rack with sea salt and a good grind of pepper. Add the racks to the pan, fat-side down and sear until golden brown; then turn the racks and brown the sides. This should take 3 – 4 minutes. Cook in batches if necessary, and allow to rest for three minutes.

6. Generously coat all sides of the racks with Dijon mustard then press each one into the herb-crumb mixture, ensuring each rack is well coated. Transfer back to the ovenproof fry pan and roast in the oven for eight minutes.

7. Remove the lamb and leave to rest for five minutes.

8. When serving, heat some red wine jus, cut the potatoes into rounds and place in the centre of each plate. Cut the racks into three chops and place on top of the dauphinoise. Spoon some jus around the plate and serve.

Linguine gamberoni

Teaming tomato based sauces with fish is typically a southern Italian fancy. Here there is something very gratifying about the tincture of torn basil, radiant pink prawns and brilliance of deep orange tinged strands of pasta. Buy the largest, freshest prawns you can.

Serves   6

Ingredients:

400g raw tiger prawns, peeled

50ml olive oil

2 large garlic cloves, peeled and crushed

A handful of flat-leaf parsley, roughly chopped

1 medium chilli, deseeded and finely chopped

75ml dry white wine

300g pomodoro sauce *(see page 168)*

2 shallots, peeled and very finely chopped

400g dried linguini

Sea salt and freshly ground black pepper

Fine cooking salt

Method:

1. Bring well-salted water to the boil in a large saucepan, ready for the pasta.

2. Heat the oil in a deep sauté pan, which has a lid, and sweat the shallots, garlic, chilli and parsley on a low heat, stirring constantly.

3. Add the white wine, cook out for a minute, then add the pomodoro sauce and reduce the liquid for about six minutes.

4. Cook the pasta for about 6−8 minutes.

5. Add the prawns to the reduced sauce, lid the sauté pan and cook for a further two minutes on a low heat. The prawns are cooked when they turn from brown-grey to pale pink, at this point remove the lid

6. Drain the linguini, rinse with freshly boiled water and shake any excess water away. Drizzle with a little olive oil, running it through the strands to prevent sticking. Add the pasta to the sauce, mix well. Heat through thoroughly and serve immediately.

Linguine vongole

Vongole is essentially a simple dish to prepare. The hardest part is obtaining the baby clams. However, nowadays most fishmongers and supermarkets do stock them in season. Ingredient bases for this dish vary from region to region, most commonly offered are 'rosso' or 'bianco'. Rosso is a tomato based sauce and bianco is without tomatoes. The latter is by far the torch bearer for me.

I've eaten this dish all over Italy, but never was it as pleasing as at the Grand Hotel Timeo in Taormina, Sicily. It was so exceptional I could have wept. I ate it twice a day for a week!

Serves   6

Ingredients:

1kg fresh clams, washed

500g dry linguine

75ml extra virgin olive oil

5 cloves of garlic, thinly sliced

1 small, hot red chilli, deseeded and very finely chopped

1 tbsp finely chopped flat-leaf parsley

50ml dry white wine

25g salted butter

Fine cooking salt

Method:

1. Bring a large pan of well-salted water to the boil and cook the pasta for five minutes. The pasta will still be a tad hard, but it will be cooked again.

2. In a sauté pan, heat the olive oil and fry the garlic and chilli until they sizzle, turn the heat down and cook until soft without browning (around two minutes). Add the parsley and remove from the heat.

3. Drain the pasta and rinse with boiling water. Drizzle a little olive oil through the strands to prevent sticking and set aside.

4. Add the clams and white wine to the empty pasta pan, cover and cook over a high heat for a few minutes, tossing a few times until the clams have opened. Once open, add the garlic and chilli mix to the pan and toss through. Add the linguine and toss the contents of the pan a few times to mix the pasta and sauce well. Cook for a further three minutes.

5. Remove from the heat, add the butter and give a final toss until the butter is melted. Serve immediately

Pan-fried calves' liver with caramelised shallots, mashed potatoes and red wine jus

Now here's a dish we served endlessly during Aqua's halcyon beginnings. It has been resurrected and incorporated in this book for a friend, who we buy in calves' liver for when he books for dinner (we also have to make him custard, but that's another story.) So, for the love of Tony Miles 'Smiley', this one's for you.

Serves   6

For the calves' liver and caramelised shallots:

18 rashers thinly sliced pancetta

1kg calves' liver, thinly sliced into 12 pieces

6 large banana shallots, thinly sliced

650ml red wine jus *(see page 167)*

40g seasoned plain flour

175ml olive oil

45g butter

1 tsp soft brown sugar

20ml good balsamic vinegar

Sea salt flakes and freshly ground black pepper

For the mash:

1kg Desirée potatoes, all approximately the same size and peeled

120ml double cream

Splash of whole milk

50g butter

Sea salt and freshly ground pepper

Method:

1. Pre-heat the oven to 190°C/Gas 5. Lay the pancetta slices on a parchment-lined baking tray, topped with another piece of parchment paper, with another baking tray on top to keep it flat and bake until crisp and dry, checking the pancetta after five minutes. Once crisp, cool on a wire rack. Set aside.

2. Boil the potatoes in well-salted water for 15 minutes until cooked, test with a knife. Drain, and press the potato flesh through a ricer into the same pan used for boiling. Heat through for a couple of minutes then remove the pan from the heat, beat in the cream and butter until smooth. Season to taste, keep warm until needed.

3. Heat the red wine jus in a medium pan and keep on a low simmer until ready to serve.

4. Heat 45g butter in a frying pan and when melted, add the sugar and shallots and gently fry on a medium heat until they turn deep brown, about 8 – 10 minutes. Add the balsamic vinegar and reduce for a minute. Remove from the heat but keep the onions warm until needed.

5. Place the seasoned flour in a large plastic bag. Pat the liver slices with kitchen towel to remove any blood then one-by-one drop them into the bag, tossing gently to ensure they are evenly coated. Shake any excess flour from the meat, and place on a plate.

6. Heat the olive oil in a large frying pan. Only add extra oil during frying if the pan becomes very dry. If there is too much oil the liver will not crisp. When hot add the liver slices three at a time and cook on each side for no more than one minute. The liver should be pink inside, slightly crisp and browned on the outside. Of course, fry the liver a little longer if you're not a fan of rare meat.

7. Place a portion of the mashed potato in the centre of each plate. Top with two slices of the liver. Spoon a dessertspoon of the caramelised shallots over the liver, place two rashers of pancetta over them and pour red wine jus around the mash liberally.

Pan-fried sea bass with risotto Milanese

This creamy, golden unrivalled classic of risotto's in its simplest version is a wonderful vegetarian dish on its own, though the addition of sea bass springs it into another league.

I am aware that bone marrow is not the easiest of ingredients to obtain. If you're struggling to find it, just omit it.

Serves   6

For the sea bass:

12 medium sea bass fillets

25g salted butter

2 tsp double cream

Juice of 2 lemons

50ml extra virgin olive oil

Sea salt and freshly ground black pepper

A little plain flour

For the risotto:

200g risotto rice

1.2 litres hot chicken stock

200g salted butter

2 tbsp bone marrow *(ask an obliging butcher)* or 100ml olive oil

½ tsp powdered saffron *(or 2 tsp saffron strands)*

1 large onion, very finely chopped

1 fat garlic clove, crushed

100g Parmesan cheese

175ml good dry white wine

Zest of 1 lemon

Method:

1. Heat 75g of the butter and the bone marrow (if using) or 100ml olive oil in a deep sauté pan over a medium heat, sauté the saffron powder (or strands) to release their flavour. Then add the onion and sauté until translucent. Add the garlic and mix well. Add the rice and stir thoroughly until each grain is coated then add 100ml of the hot chicken stock. Keep stirring the rice until the stock has disappeared. When the stock has been absorbed, repeat the process, ladle by ladle, until there are only a couple of ladles left. At this point, add the lemon zest and wine and reduce until all the liquid has been absorbed. Then add the remaining stock and cook on a lower heat for about 10–15 minutes, with the lid on, until creamy.

2. Whilst the risotto is cooking, heat 75g of butter and the olive oil in a frying pan over a medium to high heat. Dust the skin side of each bass fillet with seasoned flour and shallow-fry, skin side down, for about 2–3 minutes until the skin is golden, then turn them. The flesh side should only be cooked for a minute to colour them.

3. Remove the risotto from the heat and stir half the Parmesan through the rice. Replace the lid on the pan and leave until ready to serve.

4. When all the fillets are cooked, transfer them to a plate, keep warm and reserve the pan.

5. Place the pan back onto a medium heat, add the lemon juice and 25g of butter and heat until bubbling, then reduce the heat and add the cream. Whisk in well and keep warm.

6. Run the remaining butter and Parmesan through the risotto until melted and spoon a portion of the rice onto pre-warmed plates. Place two fillets, skin-side up on top of the risotto and spoon the lemon sauce both around the risotto and on top of the fillets. Serve immediately.

Pollo farcito

I use low moisture mozzarella, which has a moisture content of less than 50 per cent. This type of cooking mozzarella is widely used for its excellent melting consistency in dishes that require the cheese to be heated without becoming watery. Crispy fried onions are better pre-bought for this recipe as they have the moisture extracted prior to frying, making them extremely crisp. Not to mention very convenient.

Serves 6

You will need a deep fat fryer and a cook's thermometer.

Ingredients:

6 chicken breasts, roughly 225g each

250g low moisture mozzarella *(see above)*

100ml fresh basil pesto *(see page 168)*

350g good, dried breadcrumbs *(such as Barts, or homemade)*

300g plain flour

4 large eggs, beaten

½ tsp maize

1.2 litres vegetable oil *(for deep fat frying)*

6 lemon wedges *(optional)*

For the spaghetti:

450g dried spaghetti

5 spring onions

70g freshly grated Parmesan

75g dried, crisp fried onions *(see above)*

100ml extra virgin olive oil

35g butter

Handful torn basil leaves

Juice of 2 lemons

Zest of 1 lemon

Sea salt flakes and freshly ground black pepper

Some fine cooking salt

Method:

1. Add the vegetable oil to the deep-fat fryer and heat to 175°C. (Please follow the manufacturer's guidelines regarding the amount of oil that can be safely accommodated in your fryer.)

2. Put a large pan of well-salted water on to boil, pre-heat the oven to 180°C/ Gas 4 and line a baking sheet with parchment paper.

3. Set up the crumbing station, using four large plates in a row. On plate one: add flour, maize and season well; on plate two: the beaten eggs; on plate three: the breadcrumbs. The fourth plate is for the crumbed chicken ready for frying.

4. Once the station has been prepared, make the stuffing. Grate the mozzarella into a mixing bowl. Add the pesto and season.

5. Remove the small fillet from the chicken breast (the fillet is on the underside of the breast, a small flap of tender meat, which detaches easily. These will not be used, so just freeze them.) Make a small, diagonal incision – no more than 2.5cm – through the thickest part of the breast. Do not slice the breast through. Now wiggle the knife around inside the breast to make a cavity for the stuffing.

6. Push as much stuffing as possible into the cavity, then work the stuffing down the breast with the back of a teaspoon. Keep doing this until each cavity has been filled but not to bursting.

7. Press each breast into the seasoned flour, ensuring complete coverage, then roll them through the egg wash. Finally, press into the breadcrumbs. Shake off any excess crumbs and place on the fourth plate. Repeat the process with the remaining breasts. Once the deep-fat fryer reaches optimum temperature begin to fry the breasts. Fry them individually for 3–4 minutes, until golden brown. Once fried, place them on the lined baking tray and cook in the oven for a further 6 minutes. Check they are cooked by inserting a cook's thermometer into the centre of the breast, avoiding the stuffing. The thermometer should read no less than 75°C.

8. While the chicken is in the oven, place the spaghetti in the pan of boiling water for 6–8 minutes. Meanwhile, heat a sauté pan on a medium to high heat, add the olive oil, melt the butter and sauté the spring onions briefly. Add the lemon juice and zest and simmer for a minute. Drain the spaghetti and immediately put it in the sauté pan (still wet). Cook for one minute, then remove the pan from the heat and stir in the Parmesan, crisp fried onions and torn basil. Arrange a portion of spaghetti on pre-warmed plates, add the fried chicken, sprinkle with sea salt and serve with Parmesan and lemon wedges (optional).

Pan-fried duck breast with cherry and balsamic jus

For this recipe, we use Magret duck breasts, which means that the breasts have been removed from the bone, without wings. They can be bought with or without skins. These breasts come vacuum packed and can be ordered either from a reputable butcher or online at www.frenchclick.co.uk.

Serves   6

Ingredients:

6 Magret duck breasts, roughly 220g each, skin on

750g butternut squash, skinned, deseeded and cubed, about 3cm square

2 level tsp Chinese five spice

100ml good balsamic vinegar

1.25 litres red wine jus *(see page 167)*

30ml groundnut oil

20g unsalted butter

2 tins stoned black cherries, drained with juices reserved

Sea salt and freshly ground black pepper

Method:

1. Heat the oven to 200°C/Gas 6. Heat the balsamic vinegar and juice from the cherry tins in a saucepan over a high heat and reduce the liquid by half. Reduce the heat, add the cherries and red wine jus to the reduction and simmer for six minutes. Remove from the heat, pop the lid on and set aside until needed.

2. Place the butternut squash in a roasting tray and pour the groundnut oil over, sprinkle with the five spice and season well. Roast for about 30 minutes, until the edges become brown and they are caramelised underneath. Remove from the heat and keep warm until needed.

3. To prepare the duck breasts, score the skins lightly, being careful not to cut into the flesh. Heat a large oven-proof frying pan over a medium to high heat, place the duck breasts in skin side down and cook until golden brown, no oil or fat is needed. Do this in two batches to ensure good airflow for browning. Drain away any excess fat that seeps out during the browning process. Turn them over and seal the flesh side for a minute, then place all the breasts into the pan and put them in the oven for about eight minutes. Remove from the oven and allow to rest for eight minutes before serving.

4. Re-heat the cherry jus. Spoon the squash onto pre-warmed serving plates. Diagonally slice the duck breasts into two, spoon the cherry jus around and over the duck breast and serve immediately.

Pollo Milanese

I can't put a number on the times I've cooked this dish at home. In fact, I told the family they really had to ask for other things, as I was beginning to develop a tic!

I've never met anyone who doesn't like this dish, it's simple, and children love it.

Serves 8

Ingredients:

8 chicken breast supremes *(i.e. with the wing bone attached)*

600g fresh white breadcrumbs or 400g of good, dried breadcrumbs

5 eggs, beaten

300g plain flour

40ml olive oil

500g dried spaghetti

100g fresh Parmesan

½ tsp ground maize

500ml pomodoro sauce *(see page 168)*

2 limes, quartered

600ml rapeseed oil

Sea salt and freshly ground black pepper

Lime segments *(optional)*

Some fine cooking salt

Method:

1. Begin by 'banging out' the chicken breasts: place each breast, one at a time, in a clean plastic bag or between two sheets of cling film, and using a meat hammer, begin to lightly bang them out until they are 1cm thick. Place the hammered breasts on a large plate.

2. Set up the crumbing station, using four large plates in a row. On plate one: add flour, maize and season well; on plate two: the beaten eggs; on plate three: the breadcrumbs. The fourth plate is for the crumbed chicken ready for frying.

3. Before beginning to crumb, put a large pan of well-salted water on to boil for the pasta.

4. Press each breast into the seasoned flour, ensuring the chicken has been completely coated. Then roll them through the egg wash before pressing into the breadcrumbs. Shake off any excess crumbs and place on the fourth plate. Repeat the process with the remaining breasts. Try not to put the breaded breasts on top of each other if not frying immediately, as they may become damp, which may result in an uneven, 'patchy' crumb crust when cooked.

5. Cook the pasta in the boiling water for 6−7 minutes, drain and run some olive oil through to prevent sticking. Set aside and keep warm until serving.

6. In a large sauté pan, start heating the pomodoro sauce gently.

7. Heat the rapeseed oil in a wide, deep sauté pan. To test if the oil is ready, drop a pinch of the breadcrumbs into the oil; if they fizz immediately, the oil is ready. Fry each breast for 2−3 minutes each side, until golden brown. When each breast is cooked, place on a large plate lined with kitchen paper and keep warm.

8. When frying the last chicken breast, pour boiling water over the pre-cooked pasta to eliminate any starch and drain well. Tip the pasta into the heated pomodoro sauce, turning to coat evenly. Cook through for about two minutes, until hot.

9. Place a chicken breast on each plate and twirl out a cone of the spaghetti pomodoro beside it. Serve with a quarter lime segment and grated Parmesan cheese.

Risotto di zucca

This is a lovely autumnal risotto. The vegetable markets in Italy at this time are a bustling feast of vibrant colours and flavours, omnipresent are the squash, very popular for their sweetness and depth of flavour, evoking an unequalled sense of comfort as the cooler nights draw in.

Serves   6

Ingredients:

850g orange pumpkin or squash

2 large garlic cloves, peeled and thickly sliced

350g Arborio risotto rice

125ml olive oil

1 litre chicken stock, hot

150g butter

¼ tsp ground nutmeg

¼ tsp ground cinnamon

1 medium onion, peeled and very finely chopped

100ml dry vermouth

100g fresh Parmesan, grated

1 bunch fresh marjoram

Sea salt and freshly ground black pepper

Method:

1. Pre-heat the oven to 220°C/Gas 7. Without peeling, cut the squash into large chunks, scraping away the seeds or fibres and place skin-side down on a baking sheet. Add the herbs and garlic, season, sprinkle with the spices and drizzle with 100ml olive oil. Cover with foil and bake for 15 minutes, then remove the foil and bake for a further 20 minutes.

2. The squash are cooked when they have begun to brown and caramelise. Remove from the oven and allow to cool. Once cooled, scrape the flesh from the skins into a bowl and reserve the juices in the tray.

3. Heat 100g of butter and the remaining 25ml of oil in a large, sturdy sauté pan and fry the onion until soft. Add the rice, stirring until each grain of rice is coated. Cook this out for two minutes, then add 100ml of hot chicken stock, simmer and stir continually until the rice has absorbed nearly all the liquid. Continue to add stock, a ladle at a time, stirring as each addition is absorbed. After about 20 minutes nearly all the stock will have been absorbed and the rice should look creamy. Add the vermouth, lid the pan and rest the rice for five minutes.

4. Add the remaining butter to the risotto in small cubes. Then add the squash flesh, reserved juices and Parmesan and gently fold into the rice. Serve immediately.

Risotto verde with Saint Agur

This is a perfect early summer risotto, showcasing the season's finest crops. The Saint Agur's gentle, nutty flavour and acidic qualities are the perfect accompaniment and deeply satisfying.

Serves   6

Ingredients:

500g asparagus, trimmed

6 shallots, peeled and finely diced

2 garlic cloves, crushed

200g pre-cooked petit pois

350g risotto rice

1 litre hot vegetable stock

100ml dry white wine

150g Saint Agur

40ml olive oil

150g unsalted butter

A handful fresh basil leaves

Sea salt and freshly ground black pepper

Method:

1. Cut the tips of the asparagus off diagonally, 5cm from the tip and keep to one side. Now slice the remaining spears into two pieces diagonally.

2. Heat 100g of butter and the olive oil together in a large sauté pan and sauté the shallots and garlic over a medium heat for three minutes, stirring frequently. Add the asparagus spears (not the tips) and cook for a further two minutes. Remove from the heat and add the rice, coating each grain with the shallots. Return to the heat, add 100ml of hot vegetable stock and stir until all the liquid has absorbed. Add the wine and continue to stir until absorbed. Continue to add the remaining stock a ladle at a time until each addition has been completely absorbed, stirring continuously.

3. Continue cooking over a low heat for about 15 – 20 minutes until all the stock has been added and the rice has become creamy and al dente. Add the asparagus tips and peas, gently fold them through the rice and cook for a further five minutes, this time, do not stir.

4. Once the risotto is cooked, remove from the heat, add the Saint Agur, and basil, folding them through rather than stirring. Season, then put the lid on the pan and rest for five minutes before serving.

Pan-seared salmon with beetroot and horseradish remoulade and rocket pesto

Salmon and beetroot are perfect partners. Try marinating the salmon overnight in beetroot juice for vivid, instant glamour to impress. Many elements of this dish can be made in advance for a quick midweek supper.

Serves 6

Ingredients:

6 salmon fillets, about 200g each, skin on

For the remoulade:

1 tiger beetroot for garnish *(optional)*

3 medium beetroot, peeled, raw

375g celeriac, peeled

1 large garlic clove, blanched & crushed

175g crème fraiche

1 heaped tsp Dijon mustard

2 tsp of freshly grated horseradish

Juice of ½ lemon

Pinch caster sugar

4–6 tbsp extra virgin olive oil for frying

Sea salt flakes

Freshly ground black pepper

For the pesto:

200g fresh rocket

3 large garlic cloves, peeled and roughly chopped

Juice and zest of ½ a lemon

50g freshly grated Parmesan cheese

50g pine kernels

150ml extra virgin olive oil

Sea salt flakes

Freshly ground black pepper

Method:

1. Pre-heat the oven to 200°C/Gas 5, line a baking tray with parchment paper and toast the pine kernels until golden brown.

2. Place the rocket, warm pine kernels, chopped garlic cloves and half the olive oil in a food processor with the blade attachment and pulse coarsely. Now add the lemon juice, zest and remaining oil and pulse until coarse but blended. Add the Parmesan and give three quick pulses. Season, decant to a jar or bowl and refrigerate until ready to use.

3. Using a mandolin or julienne blade on a food processor, shred the celeriac into matchsticks, do the same with the beetroot, (except the tiger beetroot, which is needed for optional decoration.) Set these aside.

4. In a large mixing bowl, lightly whisk the crème fraiche, mustard, grated horseradish, lemon juice, crushed garlic, caster sugar and two pinches of sea salt flakes.

5. Add the celeriac and beetroot matchsticks to the crème fraiche mixture, combine well and refrigerate until needed.

6. To sear the salmon, pat the salmon fillets dry with kitchen towel. Make two small cuts to the skin side using a sharp knife and season the skins well.

7. Heat half the olive oil in a sturdy, non-stick frying pan/skillet over a medium to high heat until hot. Place the fillets skin side down in the pan for 4 – 5 minutes until golden brown and crisp. Do not attempt to move the fillets around in the pan, as you will damage the searing process. Turn the fillets over to colour for one minute, as they should be just pink inside, that is, medium rare. I suggest cooking three fillets at a time to help the air flow.

8. Slice the tiger beetroot very thinly with a mandolin and serve the salmon immediately, topped with the rocket pesto and a hearty portion of the remoulade topped with a slice of tiger beetroot.

Roast cod with a parsley crust, garlic mash potato and creamed leeks

I have to admit this recipe is a rough adaptation of a Gordon Ramsay recipe that I adore. I find it easy to prepare and a brilliant technique for poaching fish. It is light, velvety and smooth, just like Gordon, not that I'm crawling, at all!

Serves 8

Ingredients:

8 thick cod fillets, 150g each, skin on and trimmed neatly

For the parsley crust:

400g fresh white bread crumbs

400g unsalted butter

150g fresh flat-leaf parsley

50g fresh chives

Zest of 3 lemons

4 tbsp whole grain mustard

Sea salt and freshly ground pepper

For the poaching liquor:

60ml olive oil

1 bay leaf

4 sprigs thyme

400ml fresh water

For the garlic mash potato:

6 large Maris Piper potatoes, peeled and evenly cubed, 2.5cm squared

7 garlic cloves, peeled

350ml whole milk

75g diced butter

125ml double cream

30ml olive oil

Sea salt and freshly ground pepper

For the creamed leeks:

8 baby leeks, trimmed and very finely sliced

150g butter

400ml double cream

Method:

The parsley crust:

1. Place the breadcrumbs and the butter in a food processor and pulse until blended. Add the lemon zest and herbs, season and pulse again for a minute. Line a large cutting board with cling film, tip the crumb mixture out, and spread roughly, cover with another piece of cling film. Roll the mixture out like pastry to 1cm thick. Transfer to a slim baking tray and place in the freezer for a couple of hours to firm up.

The garlic potato purée:

1. Boil the potatoes in salted water for 15 minutes or until a knife slips easily through them, then drain. Press through a ricer into the pan, put the lid on at an angle to release condensation and set aside.

2. To blanch the garlic, put a small pan of well-salted water on to boil and prepare a small bowl of iced water. Boil the garlic cloves in the pan for 30 seconds. Remove with a slotted spoon and plunge them into the iced water. Repeat the process twice more. Then press through a garlic crusher into the riced potatoes. In the pan used for the garlic, heat the milk and cream until soft bubbles appear around the edges, then gently stir this into the potato. until very smooth, season and remove from the heat. Add the butter little by little until well-blended. Cover with a damp tea towel and keep warm until needed.

Cooking & assembly:

1. Pre-heat the oven to 200°C/Gas 6.

2. Take the crust out of the freezer and cut into squares that match the dimensions of the cod. Spread the mustard on the skin side of each fillet. Lay a piece of the crumb crust on the mustard and press down firmly. Place the fillets in an ovenproof dish about 10cm deep.

3. In a medium pan, bring 400ml water, the oil and herbs to the boil, remove from the heat and gently pour down the side of the dish, ensuring not to let any water touch or reach the crusts of the fillets. Bake for 8 – 10 minutes.

4. Melt 150g butter in a saucepan and sweat the leeks until very soft. Add the cream, season and cook for two minutes. Turn the heat down and keep warm until needed.

5. Warm the potato purée and spoon portions onto pre-warmed plates.

6. With a slotted, flat fish slice, gently remove the fillets from the poaching dish. While the fillet is still on the fish slice, drain briefly on kitchen paper and then place on top of the potato puree, spoon the creamed leeks around and serve.

Roast ray wings with basil caper butter and toasted crumbs, served with palline di patate piccolo

My family owned a famous fish and chip shop in Marylebone Lane, London, 'The Golden Hind' for 52 years, and I'm glad to report, it's still operational. My father would eat ray wings three nights a week, so skate and rays have fascinated me ever since. I can remember my uncle Aldo saying that ray was one of the only fish that needs to be medium to well done. For the longer you cook ray, the more tender it becomes.

Serves   6

For the ray wings:

6 ray wings, on the bone, about 350g each

3 tbsp plain flour

75ml dry vermouth

75g unsalted butter

90g fresh white bread crumbs

Juice of 1 lemon

1 bunch of flat leaf parsley

20ml double cream

Sea salt flakes and freshly ground black pepper

For the basil caper butter:

100g unsalted butter, softened

Zest of 1 lemon

1 tsp finely chopped parsley

1 dsp finely chopped basil

1 dsp of finely chopped capers

For the palline patate piccolo:

4kg potatoes, peeled

300g clarified butter

Sea salt flakes and freshly ground black pepper

Method:

1. Pre-heat the oven to 180°C/Gas 4.

2. Prepare a medium bowl of water. One by one, carve small balls of raw potato from the flesh, using a melon baller, ensuring the balls are solid and spherical. Once achieved, place the balls into the bowl with some salt and set aside.

3. Prepare the caper butter by mixing the butter, capers, herbs and lemon zest together and set aside until needed.

4. Place the breadcrumbs on a parchment-lined baking tray and cook in the oven until dried, but not coloured. Melt 25g of the butter and rub into the breadcrumbs before placing the tray back in the oven, cooking until golden.

5. Turn the oven up to 200°C/Gas 5. Grease a baking tray large enough to take all the wings and set aside.

6. Heat a knob of butter in a large frying pan over a medium to high heat. Dust the wings with well-seasoned flour and fry in batches of two at a time, presentation side down first. Once golden brown, turn them over to colour the other side, then transfer to the baking tray, presentation side up and set aside.

7. Heat the clarified butter in a large deep frying pan over a medium heat. Drain the potato balls and dry them with kitchen towel. Place the balls in the pan in a single layer and shake gently to coat them thoroughly. It is important to swirl the balls about the pan to keep the surfaces evenly cooked. The potatoes are ready when they are an even golden brown and tender inside, this should take about 8 minutes. Once cooked, keep the potatoes warm in the oven.

8. Meanwhile, put the ray wings in the oven to finish them for about eight minutes. Take them out and spread a dessertspoon of the basil and caper butter evenly on each wing, then back in the oven for a further two minutes.

9. Remove the ray wings from the tray onto a warming plate. Place the tray with the juices on the hob over a high heat, add the vermouth and reduce this down. When it starts to bubble and thicken, add the parsley and cream and remove from the heat.

10. Place a ray wing on each serving plate. Divide the potato balls into equal portions and plate up. Spoon the sauce around the ray wings and scatter the breadcrumbs over or serve separately in a bowl.

Smoked haddock and leek risotto

Although traditionally tail ends and off cuts from the main fish were used for this risotto, nowadays, thankfully, chefs use the best undyed smoked haddock. The very yellow smoked haddock is painted with a dye called quinoline yellow (E104) and have never actually undergone any smoking process.

The best smoked haddock is Arbroath smokies. They originate from a small fishing village called Auchmithie; where legend has it they were created after a building containing barrels of haddock preserved in salt caught fire, destroying its contents. Upon the villagers' morning inspection of the damage, the barrels with the haddock were discovered to be harbouring lovely smoked fish!

Serves 6

Ingredients:

3 undyed smoked haddock fillets

300g Arborio rice

4 leeks, cleaned and trimmed, cut into 1.5cm slices

125g baby spinach, washed

125g pre-cooked and shelled broad beans

Zest of ½ a lemon

2 dsp mascarpone cheese

125g butter

100ml olive oil

300ml whole milk

500ml vegetable stock, hot

2 sprigs thyme

1 bay leaf

1 garlic clove, thinly sliced

4 black pepper corns

100g Parmesan

Sea salt flakes and freshly ground black pepper

Method:

1. Pre-heat the oven to 190°C/Gas 5.

2. Place the haddock, skin side down in a deep baking tray. Pour the milk down the side of the tray and scatter the peppercorns, bay leaf, thyme, sliced garlic and 25g of the butter on the fillets. Cover with tin foil and bake for 10−12 minutes or until the fish flesh comes away from the skin easily. Once cooked, move the fish onto a plate, remove the skin, flake into hearty pieces and cool. Strain the milky fish stock into a bowl and set aside.

3. Melt 75g of the butter and the oil in a sturdy sauté pan and begin to sweat the leeks on a medium heat. Once translucent, add the rice, stir around until each grain is coated and cook this out for two minutes. Add 100ml of the hot vegetable stock, and simmer, stirring until the rice has absorbed nearly all the liquid. Then add the milky fish stock a ladle at a time and cook until absorbed. Continue to add more of the vegetable stock as each addition is absorbed. After about 15−20 minutes, nearly all the stock will have been absorbed.

4. Add the remaining butter to the rice, fish flakes, broad beans, spinach, mascarpone and the lemon zest and cook for two minutes then remove from the heat. Fold the Parmesan in, being careful not to over-stir. Place a lid on the pan and allow to stand for five minutes before serving.

Spaghetti with pancetta, shallot purée, toasted breadcrumbs and endive salad

Another common southern Italian practice is to use toasted breadcrumbs in cooking. It derives from cheeses either not being readily available or the poor not being able to afford cheese, or both! So breadcrumbs were used as a substitute.

I just love this dish's simplicity, flavours and textures.

Serves 6

For the spaghetti:

400g dried spaghetti

250g fresh white breadcrumbs

100ml extra virgin olive oil

3 banana shallots, very finely diced

Zest of ½ a lemon

75g butter

1 small bunch parsley, very finely chopped

400g pancetta lardons, finely diced

For the endive salad:

6 endives, cored, leaves separated

2 egg yolks

200g dolcelatte cheese

1 tbsp Dijon mustard

2 tbsp sherry vinegar

2 tsp fresh lemon juice

2 tbsp crème fraîche

235ml extra virgin olive oil

Sea salt and freshly ground pepper

Method:

1. Place the egg yolks, dolcelatte, vinegar, mustard and lemon juice in a food processor bowl, and pulse. As the mixture blends, very, very slowly add the olive oil – a constant trickling action is needed. After all the oil has been added the dressing should have a smooth mayonnaise-like consistency. Transfer the dressing to a bowl and combine with the crème fraîche, season to taste and set aside.

2. Bring a large pan of well-salted water to the boil for the pasta.

3. Heat the oven to 180°C/Gas 4. Spread the breadcrumbs evenly on a baking sheet lined with parchment paper and toast in the oven until pale golden brown. Set aside.

4. Fry the pancetta in a deep frying pan until crisp and golden brown. Remove with a slotted spoon and place on a plate with kitchen paper until ready to use.

5. In the same pan, gently sauté the shallots with half the olive oil and 25g of the butter, for about 15 minutes, until very soft. Transfer to a mixing bowl and purée using a hand blender. Set aside.

6. Cook the pasta in the boiling water for about eight minutes. Meanwhile, arrange the endive leaves on a dish and drizzle liberally with the dressing.

7. Wipe out the frying pan with kitchen towel and melt 40g of butter over a medium heat. Fry the toasted breadcrumbs until golden brown then place on a plate with kitchen towel.

8. Drain the pasta then transfer straight into the frying pan. Add a knob of butter, the shallot purée, pancetta, lemon zest and parsley. Tong this through thoroughly and fry for a few minutes until hot. Transfer the spaghetti to a large serving bowl, scatter the breadcrumbs over and serve immediately with the endive salad.

Squid ink risotto with a chive mascarpone

This is a Venetian dish, and in Venice's vibrant markets squid are often bought with their ink sack attached. Not so easily found that way over here. I buy ink sachets from www.melburyandappleton.co.uk, but many delicatessens stock them now. Adding squid ink to the rice, delicately imparts an evenness to the dish, which would otherwise be absent.

Serves   6

For the risotto:

24 fresh baby squid, cleaned with tentacles removed but retained

1 – 1.25 litres shellfish stock, hot *(see page 171)*

2 plump garlic cloves, crushed

4 – 5 squid ink sachets

4 medium shallots, finely diced

300g risotto rice

75ml dry white wine

150g fresh Parmesan, grated

200g butter

100ml olive oil

300ml groundnut oil

A little plain flour, for dusting

Sea salt and freshly ground black pepper

For the chive mascarpone:

500g mascarpone cheese

1 large bunch chives, finely chopped

Sea salt and freshly ground black pepper

Method:

1. Add the chopped chives to the mascarpone mix well and season to taste. Transfer to a bowl, cover and refrigerate until needed.

2. In a deep frying pan, heat 300ml of groundnut oil.

3. Dab the squid tentacles dry. Add a little plain flour to a carrier bag and season well. Add the tentacles to the bag and shake gently until all are lightly dusted. Shake off any excess flour. Check the oil is hot by adding a pinch of flour to the pan; if the oil fizzes, it's ready. Begin to fry the tentacles until golden brown, then, using a slotted spoon, transfer them to a plate lined with kitchen paper and set aside. Sieve the oil into a jar and keep for another time. Wipe the pan clean.

4. Heat 50ml of the olive oil and 25g butter in the sauté pan, gently sweat the shallots and garlic for about eight minutes, until soft. Now add the squid and fry for a further three minutes. Remove the squid and leave the pan on the heat.

5. Add 100g of the butter and the remaining 50ml of olive oil to the pan and return it to the heat. Add the rice and mix well, until all the rice is coated. Cook out for two minutes then add 100ml of hot shellfish stock and the wine. Gently simmer, stirring constantly until all the stock has been absorbed. Add the squid ink to the rice and stir well. Keep adding stock, a ladle at a time, until each addition has been absorbed.

6. Take the pan off the heat and add 50g of butter to the risotto, add the Parmesan and fold through. Place a lid on the pan and stand for five minutes.

7. Place a portion of risotto onto pre-warmed dinner plates, and spoon a dessertspoon of the chive mascarpone in the centre of each. Decorate the dish by arranging three of the fried tentacles around the mascarpone. Serve immediately.

Veal chops with lemon potato purée and salsa verde

The practice of boiling potatoes in their skins for purees results in the potato keeping its flavour and absorbing less liquid during cooking. Once cream and milk are added the puree is smooth, rather than sloppy.

Serves 6

For the veal chops:

6 veal loin chops, trimmed, 200g each

A little olive oil

2 fresh rosemary sprigs, chopped

For the lemon purée:

1kg Desirée potatoes of similar size, unpeeled

200ml whipping cream

200ml whole milk

Zest of 2 unwaxed lemons

Sea salt and freshly ground black pepper

For the salsa verde:

5 anchovy fillets, finely chopped

1 tsp capers, finely chopped

1 large bunch fresh mint, finely chopped

1 large bunch flat leaf parsley, finely chopped

1 tsp Dijon mustard

1 garlic clove, crushed

25ml red wine vinegar

100ml olive oil

Sea salt and freshly ground black pepper

Method:

1. Using a meat hammer, begin to bang out the chops to flatten slightly. Place them on a baking sheet, brush with olive oil, sprinkle with chopped rosemary then cover with cling film and place in the fridge for two hours.

2. Add the anchovies, capers and garlic to a pestle and mortar and grind to a paste. Add the chopped herbs, mustard and vinegar and whisk. While whisking, slowly add the olive oil, then season the salsa to taste, decant to a bowl, cover and chill until needed.

3. Boil the potatoes, still in their skins, in well-salted water. Cook for 10 – 15 minutes, until soft. Once cooked, drain the water and begin to peel away the skins with your fingers (they will be hot, so wear gloves). Press the potatoes flesh through a ricer back into the pan and heat through for a minute. Heat the milk and cream slightly in a small pan, then begin to beat this into the potatoes. Cook for a further two minutes, add the lemon zest, season, combine well and remove from the heat.

4. Heat a large sturdy non-stick frying pan/griddle pan over a high heat. Season the chops and cook each side for about 7 minutes until brown, making sure to baste them with the remaining marinade while cooking.

5. Reheat the potato purée and serve immediately with the salsa verde.

Dolce

Bruléed gunpowder tea and lavender panna cotta with honey-snap biscuits

Tea, lavender and gunpowder tea form an unexpected elegance, which I hope you enjoy. The consistency you are looking for is slightly firmer than crème brulée. Vegetarians can substitute agar agar for gelatin.

Serves   8

You will need a cook's torch to brulée.

For the panna cotta:

4 leaves gelatin

850ml double cream

285ml whole milk

170g caster sugar

2 tsp loose gunpowder tea

1 tsp dried, edible lavender

12 tsp demerara sugar

1 piece of muslin

For the honey-snap biscuits:

120g granulated sugar

120g unsalted butter

4 tbsp of lavender honey

120g plain flour

Juice of 1 lemon

Good pinch ground ginger

Method:

1. Pre-heat the oven to 190°C/Gas 5. Lightly oil two baking trays and line with baking parchment.

2. Heat the butter, sugar and honey in a medium saucepan until dissolved, then remove from the heat. Sift the flour into the pan and beat until there are no lumps. Add the lemon juice and ginger and mix well.

3. Spoon six teaspoons of the mixture onto each baking tray, leaving at least 15cm between each spoonful.

4. Bake the biscuits for 5−7 minutes until golden and have a lattice like appearance. Watch them carefully, as they burn quickly. Unless you have a larger than average oven, the biscuits should be baked in two batches. Once all the biscuits are cooked, leave them to cool completely before releasing them from the baking parchment. Leave to rest on a wire rack until needed or keep in an airtight container if they are to be used later.

5. Place the gelatin in a bowl and cover with cold water. Pour the cream and milk into a large saucepan and add the caster sugar, loose tea and lavender and bring near to boiling point. Once at this point, reduce the heat to very low for two minutes, then remove from the heat and cool for five minutes. Sieve the mixture through muslin to remove the tea leaves and lavender. Pour the strained mix back into the saucepan.

6. Lift the gelatin out of the water and squeeze out any excess liquid. Add the gelatin to the milk/cream mixture and place back on a gentle heat, lightly whisking until the gelatin has completely dissolved.

7. Pour the panna cotta cream into serving glasses/vessels and refrigerate for at least four hours, preferably overnight.

8. Remove the panna cotta glasses from the fridge and serve with a honey-snap biscuit.

Chocolate parfait with coffee anglaise sauce

This is one of the first recipes I was taught by the chef who first opened Aqua with my husband. Fifteen years later we are still asked if we will reintroduce it to the menu. Of course, it's also a great dinner party dessert, as it can be made well in advance. Although a simple enough recipe to execute, it requires that you use three bain maries! So unless you want pots and pans everywhere, I suggest you set up the one large bain marie with three separate, adequately fitting bowls.

Once made, the cream anglaise also makes a great coffee ice cream. Allow the mixture to cool completely, place in an ice cream machine and follow the manufacturer's instructions.

Serves   8

You will need a 25cm terrine

For the parfait:

7 large egg yolks

100g caster sugar

175g good quality dark chocolate, at least 70% cocoa solids

600ml double cream

30 amoretti biscuits, lightly crushed

50ml Amaretto liqueur

A little groundnut oil for greasing

For the coffee anglaise sauce:

8 large egg yolks

75g caster sugar

300ml whole milk

300ml double cream

1 tsp instant coffee granules, diluted in 2 teaspoons of cold water

Method:

For the parfait:

1. Very lightly oil the terrine and line with cling film. Evenly distribute the Amoretti biscuits over its base and gently spoon the Amaretto liqueur over the biscuits until damp, but not wet.

2. Set up a bain marie pan with three separate, fitting bowls. Make sure the water level is maintained during each process – the water must not touch the bowl's base.

3. Melt the chocolate over the bain marie in the first bowl until almost melted. As soon as there are only a few small lumps left, remove the bowl from the heat - the lumps will melt away with the heat of the bowl. It's important to stress that the chocolate must not over-heat. Allow to cool slightly.

4. Using an electric whisk, whisk the egg yolks and sugar in the second bowl over the bain marie until thick and at least doubled in volume.

5. Slowly pour the cooled chocolate into the egg mixture and combine well, then pour in the cream and whisk until soft peaks form.

6. Carefully, pour the liquid parfait into the lined terrine, cover with cling film and place in the freezer.

For the coffee anglaise sauce:

1. Beat the egg yolks and sugar together until pale in the third bain marie bowl, off the heat.

2. Heat the cream and milk in a medium saucepan until small bubbles appear around the edges. Remove from the heat and add the dissolved coffee.

3. Put the bowl with the egg and sugar over the bain marie and whisk in the cream and milk mixture. It's important to whisk quickly to avoid splitting. As the egg mix warms through it will thicken to create custard. Keep stirring until it coats the back of a spoon. Remove the bowl from the heat and allow to cool. Place a piece of cling film over its surface to avoid a skin forming. Cool and refrigerate until needed.

4. Remove the terrine from the freezer and turn out onto a chopping board. Remove the cling film and cut the parfait into 2cm thick slices. Spoon a small ladle of coffee anglaise onto a cold plate. Lay the parfait slices in the sauce, slightly overlapping and serve or display as I have.

Chocolate torte with blueberry cream

There is something very serious and adult about this torte. With its intense, deeply chocolatey, fudge like texture, yet slightly bitter finish, it's not something I would serve to children. I always ponder on whether to make this cake at home for events, as I know I will be the one who ends up eating it!

Serves   10 - 12

You will need a 30cm, non-stick, loose-bottomed cake tin.

For the torte:

500g best quality plain chocolate, minimum 70% cocoa solids

500g salted butter

12 large eggs, separated

1 tsp cream of tartar

250g caster sugar

110g soft, light brown sugar

110g hazelnuts, fine-ground

6 tbsp of plain flour, sifted

For the blueberry cream:

550g fresh blueberries

700ml whipping cream

1 dsp icing sugar

Decoration:

300g crushed hazelnuts

Icing sugar for dusting

Method:

1. Pre-heat the oven to 170°C/Gas 4. Grease the cake tin and line with parchment.

2. Set up a medium bain marie, add the chocolate and butter to the bowl and begin to melt them, slowly. Don't stir it too much, allow it to melt until there are only a few small lumps left, then remove from the heat. These lumps will melt away in the heat of the liquid chocolate.

3. Whisk both sugars and the egg yolks in a bowl using an electric whisk until a very pale 'latte' colour is achieved. Set aside.

4. Clean and dry the whisk thoroughly and, in a clean, dry bowl, whisk the egg whites with the cream of tartar and a pinch of salt until stiff peaks form. Set aside.

5. Stir the chocolate into the sugar and egg yolk mix and combine well, then add the hazelnuts and flour in batches and gently stir together until there are no lumps.

6. Very gently fold the egg whites into the cake batter little by little, keeping as much air in as possible.

7. Transfer to the cake tin and bake for 50−60 minutes. It's ready when a skewer is passed through the centre and comes away clean. At this point remove the torte from the oven and allow to cool completely in the tin.

For the blueberry cream:

1. Heat the blueberries and sugar until boiling then pass the purée through a fine sieve into a medium bowl and allow to cool.

2. Pour the whipping cream into a bowl and begin to whisk with an electric whisk until thick but not fully whipped.

3. Fold the blueberry coulis into the cream until blended, cover and chill until ready to serve.

4. Before serving, generously scatter over the crushed hazelnuts and dust with icing sugar. Serve with the blueberry cream.

Sticky toffee pudding with mini toffee apples and sticky toffee sauce

This dish remains a staple on our menu. I have made the addition of mini toffee apples for texture and glamour really, also they're very easy to make and evoke such praise. Crab apples are great for these but not always in season. Alternatively, you can buy the mini apples preserved in jars from www.melburyandappleton.co.uk

Serves 8

You will need 8 x 10cm x 10cm deep non-stick individual cake tins or a 36cm x 8cm rectangular baking tin. You will also need a sugar thermometer, a pair of tweezers and a small non-stick baking tray for the apples.

For the pudding:

400g of dried pitted dates, chopped

650ml water

2 tsp of bicarbonate of soda

110g salted butter, softened, plus a little for greasing the cake tins

325g dark muscovado sugar

400g self raising flour, plus a little plain flour for dusting the tins

130ml golden syrup

130ml black treacle

2 tsp good vanilla extract

4 large eggs

For the mini toffee apples:

26 crab apples or 2 x 7.4oz jars of mini apples in caramel

250g caster sugar

100ml water

A few drops of lemon juice

For the toffee sauce:

375g soft dark brown sugar

375g salted butter, diced

800ml double cream

1 dsp vanilla extract

Method:

1. Set the oven to 200°C/Gas 6

2. To make the sticky toffee apples, combine the sugar and water in a small saucepan, add the lemon juice and cook on a medium heat without agitating the pan, (which would result in having crystals in your caramel) until the mixture begins to bubble slightly.

3. Place the thermometer into the centre of the mixture, when the reading is exactly 150°C/300°F, remove the caramel from the heat.

4. Using the tweezers, begin to dip the apples in the caramel, ensuring they are completely coated. Set them on the non-stick tray until needed.

5. Note: Work fast as the caramel begins to harden quickly! If it does become too thick to continue, return the pan to the heat, just to loosen the mix, then continue, but beware, sugar burns at an alarming speed!

6. Line the cake tins by lightly greasing them with butter and dust with plain flour. Tap away as much of the flour as you can. Line the bottom of the tins with baking parchment.

7. To make the sauce, combine the butter, sugar and cream in a sturdy saucepan. Gradually heat the mixture over a moderate heat, do not boil. Stir to check that the sugar has completely dissolved. Once dissolved allow to cool slightly before adding the vanilla extract. Loosely cover and set aside.

8. In a large bowl, cream together the butter and sugar, add the eggs one at a time, then add the golden syrup and treacle. Mix until blended, add the vanilla extract and set aside.

9. In a small saucepan, bring the dates and water to the boil, remove from the heat and let stand for three minutes.

10. While the dates are standing, begin to sift the flour into the egg batter in a couple of batches until blended.

11. Place half the date mixture into a blender and very lightly pulse until roughly chopped, not pureed! Repeat with the remaining half, then pour the mixture into a large jug, add the bicarbonate of soda and mix well. It will fizz up. Fold half the date mixture into the egg mix, then add the other half and fold again.

12. Pour the batter into the cake tins and bake for 25 minutes, add an extra 10 minutes if using one large tin. They're ready when the centres spring back to the touch. Serve with three mini toffee apples and vanilla ice cream.

Rose and pistachio torte with rose cream

See overleaf for the recipe

Rose and pistachio torte with rose cream

This is an adaptation of a dessert my mother made for me as a small child. Originally it was rose ice cream served with caramelised roasted pistachios, which I'm guessing came from her time in India. I still hold the memory of the fragrant, warm sweet nuts and the delicate perfume of the ice cream. I have tried to simulate these qualities in this torte.

Serves 10

You will need a 10 inch x 2 inch, non stick, loose bottomed flan tin. Greased and dusted with flour.

For the pastry:

220g plain flour

110g freshly, finely ground pistachio nuts

100g caster sugar

170g of unsalted butter, softened

Pinch of fine salt

2 medium egg yolks, beaten

3 desert spoons of rose petal jam

For the filling:

200g freshly ground pistachio nuts

200g caster sugar

200g unsalted butter, softened

40g plain flour

4 medium eggs, beaten

1 tbsp Briottet liqueur de Rose

For the rose cream:

350ml whipping cream

1 tbsp sifted icing sugar

2 tsp rose extract

To decorate:

300-400g, pistachio nuts, roughly ground or crushed

Pink roses petals

A little icing sugar

Method:

1. Make the pastry. Sift the flour and salt onto a clean work surface, scatter over the ground pistachios. Begin to work in the softened butter, rubbing it into the flour and nuts until a breadcrumb consistency is achieved. Make a well in the centre of the mix and add the egg yolks. Begin to draw the pastry together and press into a ball. Swiftly knead the pastry together a few times on a lightly floured surface, wrap in cling film and refrigerate for a good hour.

2. Pre-heat the oven to 180°C/Gas 4. Remove the pastry from the fridge and shape into a flat circle. Place a large piece of cling film underneath the pastry, place another piece on top and with a rolling pin begin to shape into a round, about a ¼ inch thick. It will need to be roughly 14 inches in diameter to fit the flan tray.

3. Remove the top layer of cling film and line the flan tin with the pastry. Prick the case all over with a folk, including the sides, and line the pastry with both sheets of cling film, making sure it covers the pastry's sides to prevent over browning. Then place a circle of parchment paper over and place baking beans onto the parchment.

4. Slip onto a baking tray and blind bake the case for 10 minutes. Remove from the oven, take away the baking beans and remove the parchment paper and cling film. Bake for a further 8 minutes until just browning. Then remove from the oven and allow to cool.

5. Once cool, spread the rose jam evenly across the case's base and pop in the freezer, uncovered, for half an hour.

6. Meanwhile, set a food processor up with the blade attachment (or you could do this part by hand). Place the butter and sugar into the processing bowl and run on a medium setting. When the mixture is pale and fluffy, add the eggs, one by one, with the motor running. Now add the ground pistachios, flour and the rose liqueur until combined.

7. Remove the pastry from the freezer. Pour the pistachio filling into the case and bake for 35–40 minutes, until golden and the centre is not wobbly. Remove from the oven and allow to cool completely.

8. Make the rose cream by whisking the sugar and cream with an electric hand whisk until thick but not whipped, at this point very lightly whisk in the rose extract, you're looking for a thick cream rather than whipped. Place the cream in a bowl, covered with cling film and refrigerate until ready to serve.

9. To decorate the torte, generously distribute the roughly ground pistachios over the torte and lightly dust with the icing sugar. Scatter with the rose petals.

David & Richard Smithson

David's apple strudel

"There are several varieties of paste or dough that can be used to make strudel, the original apple strudel emanates from Austria. I have chosen the following recipe because it was handed down to me by a German chef, Willey Bode. It had been passed down to him by his grandmother, who herself had been given it by an Austrian cousin during the Second World War, so its authenticity cannot be questioned.

The making of the strudel requires a little practise. The challenging element is rolling out the dough until it is so thin and elastic it is possible to see your hand through it. Good luck!"

David Smithson

See overleaf for the recipe

David's apple strudel

For the dough:

220g plain flour

1 egg, plus 1 yolk, beaten

60ml whole milk

50g butter, diced

Pinch of salt

For the filling:

5 – 10 cooking apples *(preferably Bramley)*

100g breadcrumbs *(brown or white)*

110g apricot jam

220g sultanas

110g walnuts

220g butter

50g soft, brown muscovado sugar

2 tsp ground cinnamon

Method:

For the dough:

1. Sift the flour and salt onto a work surface. Make a well in the centre. Add the diced butter and rub through the flour until a crumb-like consistency is achieved. Make another well, pour in the beaten egg, and blend to form dough. Add the milk, a little at a time, until the dough is very soft and elastic. Place in a bowl, cover with a damp tea towel and allow to stand for an hour.

For the filling:

1. Pre-heat the oven to 190°C/Gas 5. Line a flat baking tray with parchment paper. Melt 120g of the butter in a small pan, add the breadcrumbs and turn through until coated. Turn the mixture onto the baking tray and bake for 7 – 8 minutes, turning regularly, until crisp. Remove from the oven and allow to cool.

2. Peel, quarter and core the apples and cut into 1cm slices. Put the apple slices into a large mixing bowl and sprinkle with the sugar. Add the sultanas, walnuts and cinnamon and combine. Spoon in the apricot jam and mix well.

For the strudel:

1. The strudel's pastry dimensions need to be 30cm by 30cm square. To do this, lay a lightly dampened cloth on a work surface. Lightly dust your hands and rolling pin with flour. Place the dough mixture onto the cloth, and roughly shape into a flat rectangle. Roll the dough in one direction and then another by turning the cloth 90 degrees every now and then. If the dough begins to stick, lightly flour the rolling pin, do not flour the dough.

2. Once the correct dimensions have been achieved, gently release the dough from the damp cloth (if necessary, use the rolling pin to support the dough whilst releasing it). Put the dough back on the cloth.

3. The pastry now needs to be stretched until almost translucent and to cover an area approximately 45cm by 55cm. To do this, take a corner of the pastry and, whilst very gently pulling it towards you, thin the pastry using the same motion as you would gently fluffing a duvet. Do this to each corner, and then to each side, until the dough has the correct dimensions and density. Use a very light touch with this process, in order not to tear the pastry. The pastry should still be on the cloth at this point.

4. Sprinkle the baked breadcrumbs evenly over the pastry, leaving a 1½ inch edge all the way round. Carefully spoon the apple mixture into the centre of the pastry, then distribute the filling over the breadcrumbs, making sure it is even and level.

5. Melt the remaining butter and brush the pastry's edges.

6. It is extremely difficult to manipulate the pastry during the strudel-rolling, so the damp tea towel provides support. First, pick up the edge of the cloth and roll the strudel over, making sure that the cloth is peeled away before the pastry meets the filling, tucking as you go. Repeat this motion, with the tea towel supporting the strudel and peeling the cloth away as the roll forms. Two inches before you meet the finishing edge, tuck in the ends of the pastry to seal the filling, lightly pinch the dough, sealing the edges, then complete the final roll. Make sure the last sealing crease is on the underside.

7. Using the cloth, lift the strudel onto the baking tray, ensuring the sealed edge is underneath.

8. Brush the strudel all over with the remaining melted butter.

9. Bake for 35 – 45 minutes, basting with melted butter after 30 minutes. Do not open the oven before this time. The strudel is ready when it is a light golden brown, and crisp to the touch.

10. Remove from the oven and leave to rest for an hour, it should still be warm when served.

Frangelico zabaglione with orange tuiles

Possibly the most iconic of Italian desserts. I have exchanged the marsala wine for Frangelico as it's simply my favourite liqueur. Any sweet wine can be used. I've also added orange zest and spices at Christmas time with much success, a sort of Italian eggnog, only not as calorific!

See overleaf for the recipe

Frangelico zabaglione with orange tuiles

Serves   8

For the tuiles (makes 25):

2 egg whites

110g caster sugar

55g unsalted butter

55g plain flour

zest of 1 orange

For the zabaglione:

200g fresh egg yolks

200g caster sugar

350ml Frangelico liqueur

A little vegetable oil for greasing

Method:

For the tuiles:

1. Pre-heat the oven to 190°C/Gas 5. Prepare six baking sheets lightly greased with vegetable oil and lined with baking parchment.

2. Whisk the egg whites in a clean, dry mixing bowl, until stiff peaks appear. Then add the sugar a tablespoon at a time, whisk until thick and glossy.

3. Melt the butter in a medium saucepan and remove from the heat. Begin to pour the butter into the meringue mixture a little at a time, add the sifted flour and fold in. When combined, fold in the orange zest.

4. Spread long thin blades (about 3cm x 20cm) of the mix onto the parchment paper with a small palette knife, you could use a stencil if you have one. Leave a 15cm gap between the strips to allow for spreading. Bake for 5—6 minutes until golden brown.

5. Lightly oil the handle of a long wooden spoon. Begin to loosen the tuiles from the parchment while they are still fairly hot. Working quickly, while they are still warm and malleable, wind them around the spoon's handle to create a long, twisted shape. Leave to cool and harden completely. Keep in an air-tight container until ready for use.

For the zabaglione:

1. Set up a large bain marie on a soft, rolling boil.

2. Whisk the egg yolks, Frangelico and sugar in the bain marie's bowl until thick and creamy. Place the bowl over the bain marie and whisk vigorously, using a balloon whisk. Do not at any time stop whisking, as the eggs will scramble.

3. Continue cooking the zabaglione until it has at least quadrupled in volume. At this point, remove it from the heat.

4. Serve the zabaglione immediately. Pour directly into the serving glasses and garnish with tuiles.

High-baked orange & ricotta cheesecake

Dedicated to my grandmother, Mona

This recipe was originally created by my Dutch grandmother's mother-in-law, who was Greek and my grandmother passed it down to me. Granny did two things very well (at least, that I am aware of)—baked cheesecake and fish curry—she used any fish, even tinned pilchards, and it was always phenomenal. However, that's a whole other book.

The Greeks favour baked cheesecake with pastry (as, interestingly, do the Jewish and the Germans), but they use a Greek cheese called 'Mizithra' of which there are three types: fresh, sweet and sour.

My grandmother used the fresh Mizithra, I have adapted her recipe, using ricotta. I'm always asked to bake this for friends' and customers' birthdays, so I'm pretty confident you'll like the results.

See overleaf for the recipe

High-baked orange and ricotta cheesecake

Serves 16 - 18

*You will need a 30cm, loose-
bottomed, non-stick cake tin.*

For the pastry:

420g plain flour

335g softened butter

165g icing sugar *(sifted)*

2 large egg yolks

2 drops vanilla extract

A pinch of salt

For the filling:

525g caster sugar

525g unsalted butter

Zest of 10 oranges, juice of 5

15ml good vanilla extract

18 large eggs, separated

750g ricotta cheese

375g self-raising flour

15g baking powder

100g large golden sultanas

Method:

For the pastry:

1. Pre-heat the oven to 180°C/Gas 4. Sift the flour and salt onto a clean work surface and make a well in the centre. Put the softened butter, sugar, egg yolks and vanilla extract in the well and begin to draw the mixture together to make a smooth dough. Once the pastry is smooth, knead briefly (do not over-work). Return to a bowl, cover with a damp cloth and allow to rest for one hour.

2. After the hour, roll the pastry out between two sheets of cling film, leaving an extra 8−10cm overhang of the cake tin's diameter to line the sides. Once the tin is lined, prick the pastry all over with a fork, also up the sides, then chill in the tin for 40 minutes before baking.

3. Once chilled, remove the tin from the fridge; line with doubled cling film and a circle of parchment paper and blind bake using baking beans for 12−15 minutes until just beginning to brown *(don't worry, the cling film doesn't melt)*. Remove from the oven and allow to cool completely.

For the filling:

1. Beat the butter and sugar in a large bowl until pale and fluffy, then add the egg yolks one at a time. If the batter starts to split add a pinch of flour. Once the mixture is combined, add the orange zest, juice and vanilla extract and mix well. Sift in the flour and baking powder and blend. Fold in the ricotta until the mixture becomes a smooth, light batter.

2. Whisk the egg whites in a large, dry bowl until stiff peaks form, then gently fold them into the ricotta mixture, keeping as much air in as possible. When fully blended, turn out into the pastry case, leaving a gap of an inch from the top. Sprinkle the sultanas over the top at this point *(they will gently sink during cooking)*. Bake for 40−50 minutes until golden brown and slightly cracked on top. Remove from the oven and allow to cool.

3. The cheesecake is best eaten within two days. I advise keeping it at room temperature. Refrigeration makes the butter and ricotta congeal and it never quite recovers its original fluffy texture.

Chef's tip:

You may have some ricotta filling left over and, if so, it makes lovely little soufflés. Not quite as high risen, but very good nevertheless. Simply butter and caster-sugar line some small ramekins, spoon in some ricotta mix, over-filling the ramekins in the middle, then swiftly run your thumb around the inner rim's edge of the ramekins as this will facilitate a clean rise. Bake for 6−8 minutes. The soufflés should have risen and be a golden brown. Dust with icing sugar and serve quickly.

Lemon drizzle cake

Who doesn't love the zing of a good lemon drizzle cake? This one definitely delivers, it is light with an intense citrusy finish, and very moist in texture.

The cake will keep for up to 3 days in a sealed container.

Serves   10

You will need a 30cm, loose-bottomed cake tin.

For the cake:

450g unsalted butter, softened

450g caster sugar

450g ground almonds

2 tsp vanilla extract

6 large eggs

Zest of 5 lemons

Juice of 2 lemons

225g fine maize flour

1½ tsp baking powder

¼ tsp fine salt

For the lemon drizzle icing:

Juice of 5 lemons

Zest of 2 lemons

350g icing sugar

Method:

For the cake:

1. Pre-heat the oven to 160°C/Gas 3. Butter and line the cake tin.

2. Beat the butter and sugar until pale and fluffy. Add the eggs one at a time, mixing well. Fold in the almonds, flour and baking powder in batches, then the lemon juice, zest and vanilla extract.

3. Spoon the mixture into the prepared cake tin and bake for 40−50 minutes. Do not open the oven for at least 30 minutes. Check by sliding a skewer into the centre; if it comes away clean, the cake is ready. Remove from the oven and allow to cool completely in the tin.

For the lemon drizzle icing:

1. Add half the lemon juice and 100g of the sugar to a small saucepan and simmer for two minutes. Remove from the heat and allow to cool a little. Then prick the cooled cake with a skewer and spoon the sugar syrup over the surface to soak through.

2. Add the remaining lemon juice and sugar to a bowl and whisk away all the lumps. Add the lemon zest, then drizzle this over the cake's surface to achieve that crackled glaze.

Lemon posset with citrus shortbreads

Who'd have thought this elegant, old-fashioned dessert, would make such a well-deserved comeback? We sell tons of it in the restaurants; luckily it's a cinch to make. Try using it set over fruit compote, once set, brulée their tops.

Serves   6

You will need a madeleine moulding tray (or any tray mould of your choice), food processor and 6 x 175ml ramekins or attractive glasses to serve.

For the posset:

600ml double cream

Zest and juice of 2 large unwaxed lemons

150g caster sugar

For the shortbread:

90g icing sugar, plus extra for dusting

185g plain flour

60g corn flour

30g ground almonds

Zest of one orange

250g unsalted butter, cut into cubes, plus extra for greasing

½ tsp Sicilian lemon extract

Cake release spray

Method:

1. Pre-heat the oven to 180°C/Gas 4. Spray the madeleine mould with cake release spray.

For the posset:

1. Place the cream and sugar in a medium saucepan on a low heat. Slowly bring the cream to the boil and cook for three minutes at a slow simmering temperature then remove from the heat and cool.

2. Once cool, add the lemon zest and juice and whisk well. Divide the lemon posset between the ramekins or glasses and chill for three hours.

For the shortbread:

1. Sift the icing sugar, flour and corn flour into a food processor's bowl with the blade attachment, add the ground almonds and butter. Pulse until there are no visible pieces of butter left. Add the orange zest and lemon extract and pulse for a further 20 seconds. Due to the consistency of the mixture it can't be cut, it must be pressed into the madeleine moulds. But, trust me, it does make the shortest possible shortbread.

2. Bake the shortbread for 10 minutes. Remove from the oven and allow to cool. Before serving, dust with icing sugar.

Chef's tip

Feel free to infuse the shortbreads with cardamom, caraway, poppy seeds etc. as long as the addition is dry.

Soufflé

A soufflé, whether sweet or savoury, is essentially a flavoured base to which beaten egg whites are added. The heat of the oven causes the air in the egg whites to expand, which releases their proteins, and these produce that show-stopping rise. Enabling the mixture to be air-filled is essential, so I advise against using bases that have been refrigerated, as it will be difficult to incorporate the egg white because the base becomes too firm.

You can freeze uncooked soufflés, should you need to make them a day or week ahead. This is easily done: once the ramekins are filled and the tops leveled, simply place each ramekin in a large freezer bag with plenty of space, so that the bag does not touch the soufflé. Tie the bags with wire ties and place them upright in the freezer.

When they're needed, follow the same cooking instructions but add five minutes to the cooking time.

Lemon soufflés with ginger beer sherbet

Serves   8

You will need 8 x 10cm wide x 6cm deep ramekins. An ice cream maker is also needed.

For the soufflé:

75g unsalted butter, softened, and a little extra for greasing

8 tbsp caster sugar, plus 75g for dusting

9 large egg whites

675ml crème patissiere *(see below)*

Zest of 10 lemons, juice of 6

For the crème patissiere:

580ml whole milk

6 egg yolks

110g caster sugar

40g plain flour

40g corn flour

2 tsp vanilla extract

For the sherbet:

300g granulated sugar

2 tbsp fresh ginger, peeled and finely minced

1 275ml bottle Fentimans ginger beer

Zest of 4 unwaxed lemons

800ml water

75ml lemon juice

Method:

For the sherbet:

1. Combine the sugar, ginger, lemon zest and water in a saucepan on a medium heat and bring to the boil, stirring constantly. Leave on a rolling boil for seven minutes, then remove from the heat and allow to cool completely. Once cold, add the lemon juice and stir well. Place in the fridge overnight.

2. In the morning, add the ginger beer and transfer the mixture to an ice cream machine and set to make sorbet, according to manufacturer's instructions (although I've found it needs a little longer than recommended).

3. Once frozen, remove from the ice cream machine. Break the sorbet into chunks and whirl in a food processor in two batches until smooth.

4. Transfer to a chilled upright container and return to the freezer for one hour, or until firm.

For the crème patissiere:

1. Heat the milk slowly in a medium saucepan, when little bubbles appear around the edge, remove from the heat.

2. Beat the egg yolks and sugar together with an electric whisk. When the mixture is very pale and ribbon-like, sift in the flours and blend well. Pour half the milk into the egg mixture and whisk by hand until lump-free, then pour the egg mix back into the pan with the remaining milk and whisk until smooth.

3. Slowly bring to the boil, stirring constantly with a balloon whisk. It will thicken alarmingly fast, just keep whisking. It's supposed to happen! At this point, remove from the heat; it should now resemble very thick custard.

4. Cover with a damp cloth and leave to cool completely. Once cold, beat in the vanilla extract, re-cover and set aside.

For the soufflés:

1. Pre-heat the oven to 220°C/Gas 7.

2. Lightly butter the ramekins and dust with 75g of the caster sugar.

3. Whisk the egg whites in a large, dry bowl until soft peaks form. Slowly add the remaining sugar in batches until soft peaks re-form.

4. Carefully fold in the cooled crème patissiere, once combined, add the lemon zest and juice until blended. Do not over-work; keeping as much air in as possible.

5. Fill the ramekins to 1 inch above their rims, then neatly flatten their tops with a palette knife, swiftly run your thumb round the ramekins inner edge, as this will improve the rise. Place on a baking sheet and bake for 7−8 minutes.

6. Remove the soufflés from the oven. Serve immediately with the ginger beer sherbert.

Little brioche apple charlottes with orange caramel sauce

For Richard

The first time I met Richard was in London. I had been called up to manage a large function that was taking place in a private club where Richard was a director. One of many tasks that day was to line 100 dariole moulds for apple charlottes. In the midst of typical kitchen mayhem, Richard appeared to ask me if everything was going smoothly. Drawing a deep breath, I replied somewhat tensely that the temp chefs we had been sent had never made apple charlottes, neither had they ever lined a dariole mould before! Time was disappearing fast, I pointed out, which was why I was lining them, although I should have been overseeing the whole operation. Richard looked at me for a moment, then asked for an apron and told me to step aside.

I was riveted to the spot as Richard began to weave his magic. I had never seen anyone complete that particular task with such speed, precision and dexterity. 'How,' I asked, 'can you do that?' Still concentrating on the slices of bread, he replied, 'Well, when I was preparing for my final exam at college, I was tipped off that the dessert dish was going to be apple charlotte, so I spent weeks practising. He finished the last dariole mould and dusted off his hands. I swooned.

See overleaf for the recipe

Little brioche apple charlottes with orange caramel sauce

Serves   8

For the apple charlottes:

10 *(8 if large)* dessert apples, preferably Cox, peeled, cored and sliced into 8 pieces

100ml calvados

110g granulated sugar

Juice of 2 oranges, zests removed and retained

1 cinnamon stick

180g unsalted butter

3 x 400g of brioche loaves

For the caramel sauce:

240g granulated sugar

100ml water

Zest of 2 oranges *(retained from juiced oranges)*

Juice of ½ a lemon

180g unsalted butter

60ml double cream

To serve:

700g clotted cream

You will need 8 x 8 ½ cm by 5cm dariole moulds.

Method

For the apple charlottes:

1. Melt the sugar, 40g of the butter, orange juice and cinnamon stick in a medium saucepan over a medium heat until the sugar has dissolved. Add the apples and cook them down to a soft consistency. At this stage add the calvados, remove from the heat and allow to cool. Put a lid on the pan and set aside.

2. Pre-heat the oven to 200°C/Gas 6. Melt the remaining butter, lightly brush the dariole moulds to line them.

3. The brioche cutting requires some careful calculation. Slice each brioche into 1cm thick slices, then cut out the circles needed for their tops and bases. You need to achieve eight circles, slightly larger than the moulds' bases and eight slightly larger than the mould circumference's rim. Slice the remaining bread into rectangles; next brush each piece with the melted butter on both sides, being careful not to leave any unbuttered patches. Then line the moulds, don't leave any gaps between them, overlap them slightly and press firmly to seal.

4. Remove the cinnamon stick from the apple mixture and start to fill the moulds, leaving a quarter inch gap at the rim. Cover the charlottes with the remaining circles, pressing around the bread's edges to seal them well. Put the moulds on a baking sheet and bake for 15 – 20 minutes until golden brown.

For the caramel sauce:

1. Put the sugar and water in a medium saucepan and set on a low heat. Once the sugar has dissolved and the colour resembles light amber, remove from the heat and slowly add the cream, vigorously whisking all the time. Large clumps may persist for a while, but just keep beating (have faith, it will disperse!) and then return to a low heat. Add the lemon juice and orange zest and return to the heat, whisking continuously and all the lumps will disappear. Remove the pan from the heat and beat in the remaining butter. Allow to cool slightly, strain through a fine sieve, cover with cling film. Prick the film once to prevent condensation. Set aside.

2. Loosen the charlottes from the moulds by running a sharp knife around the edges. Then put the serving plate, horizontally, upside down on the top of the mould. Carefully tip the charlottes onto a plate, spoon some orange sauce over and around. Serve with clotted cream.

Marsala figs with brutti ma buoni and vanilla mascarpone

Dedicated to my time in Sorrento

Brutti ma buoni are Italian biscuits made in the same way as meringue, with chopped hazelnuts. 'Brutti ma buoni' translates literally as 'ugly but good', strange, I know, but I have seen them made with whole nuts, which does give them a rather knobbly appearance. However, trust me when I say they are delicious!

Their texture and nutty taste work beautifully with this dish. A friend of mine made these biscuits the night before she planned to test this dessert for me, only to find her family had eaten them all before the morning had come!

See overleaf for the recipe

Marsala figs with brutti ma buoni and vanilla mascarpone

Serves 8

For the marsala figs:

16 large ripe figs *(preferably black)*

150ml sweet marsala wine

Juice of 1 orange

Juice of ½ a lemon

1 level tsp icing sugar

For the brutti ma buoni biscuits (makes 20 large biscuits):

200g white granulated sugar

4 large egg whites

1½ tsp vanilla extract

75g of plain flour

125g whole raw hazelnuts

For the vanilla mascarpone:

700g mascarpone cheese

2 vanilla pods

2 tsp icing sugar, sifted

Method:

For the brutti ma buoni:

1. Pre-heat the oven to 175°C/Gas 4. Lightly brush 2−3 baking trays with oil and line with parchment paper.

2. Scatter the hazelnuts on one of the baking sheets and bake for about 10 minutes, until they become fragrant and their skins begin to flake. Remove from the oven and wrap in a clean tea towel to let them steam for 10 minutes. Then vigorously rub them in the cloth to remove their outer husks. Place in a food processor and pulse for a few seconds, until they are roughly chopped.

3. Start to heat the egg whites and sugar over a bain marie whisking constantly until they are pale and begin to thicken.

4. Remove from the heat and whisk with an electric hand whisk for five minutes. The mix will become thick and glossy and should resemble thick meringue. At this point, stir in the vanilla extract and fold in the flour and hazelnuts.

5. Place 1½ tablespoons of the mixture onto the lined baking sheets, about 5cm apart as the biscuits will spread. Bake for 20−25 minutes until pale brown. Remove from the oven and cool on wire racks. The brutti ma buoni can be made a day ahead and keep for longer in an airtight container.

For the vanilla mascarpone:

1. Tip the mascarpone into a bowl. Split the vanilla pods and scrape the seed paste from the pods. Mix the seed paste into the mascarpone along with the icing sugar, blend well and refrigerate until needed.

For the marsala figs:

1. Turn the oven up to 200°C/Gas 6. Mix the marsala wine, orange juice, lemon juice and icing sugar in a large bowl. Cut a cross, 1cm deep in the top of each fig, place in an ovenproof dish, spoon the marinade over their tops and bake for 10 minutes. Then allow to cool, cover and refrigerate overnight, basting occasionally.

2. Place two brutti ma buoni biscuit in the centre of the serving plate. Arrange two figs on each plate and drizzle some marinade over the figs and around the plate. Spoon a generous dollop of vanilla mascarpone neatly on top.

Montenegro and amaretti baked peaches with pistachio gelato

I have tried a number of pistachio gelato recipes, but none has delivered the pistachio punch I craved. Also, there was a lot of faffing around with the shelling and pulsing of nuts. Until I discovered a wonderful pistachio paste that can be bought at good delis or online: Bronte pistachio paste from Sicily, where the finest pistachios are harvested for their rich colour and intense flavour. Best of all, the paste is easy to use.

Montenegro is an intensely aromatic Italian digestif, sweet with a bitter finish, the bitterness is dispersed by sugars in the cooking, leaving a rich, botanical aroma. It works very well with both fruit and chocolate.

Serves 8

You will need an ice cream maker.

For the peaches:

8 firm ripe peaches

1 orange, juice only

50g amoretti biscuits

50g unsalted butter, diced

40g caster sugar

150ml Montenegro

140ml hot water

For the ice cream (makes 1.5 litres):

2 x 380g jars Bronte pistachio paste

4 level tsp corn flour

1 litre whole milk

100g caster sugar

A few drops of lemon juice

Method:

For the gelato:

1. Make a thin paste by mixing approximately 30ml of the cold milk with the corn flour until the paste is smooth and lump-free.

2. Heat the remaining milk and sugar in a medium saucepan. When it reaches near-boiling point (there should be small bubbles foaming around the edge of the saucepan), remove the pan from the heat and briskly whisk in the corn flour paste. Return the pan to the heat and cook out for three minutes, whisking constantly, the mixture will thicken to a custard consistency.

3. Remove from the heat and pour into a bowl to cool, then refrigerate overnight. Once chilled, whisk the pistachio paste and lemon juice into the milk custard until smooth. Then pour the custard into an ice cream machine and freeze according to manufacturer's instructions.

For the peaches:

1. Pre-heat the oven to 180°C/Gas 4. Crush the amaretti biscuits to coarse crumbs. Cut around the peaches then twist the two halves apart. Run a hulling knife (or small bladed knife) around and underneath the stones to release them, take a teaspoon and remove a little more from the peach stones' cavity. Put them, flesh side up, in an ovenproof dish, spoon a heaped dessertspoon of the amaretti crumbs into the cavity space, spilling over their tops. Place a thin slice of butter over the crumbs and sprinkle with a little of the sugar.

2. Then pour the Montenegro and orange juice into the dish, dot the remaining butter and sugar around the peaches and bake for 15 minutes until the liquid around the peaches begins to take on a golden brown, amber colour. Then add 140ml hot water to the dish and bake for a further 15 minutes until the peach tops have turned a deep golden. Remove from the oven.

3. By now there will be a fair amount of syrupy liquid in the dish. Remove the peaches, place the dish on the hob, add a knob of butter and reduce the syrup down for a couple of minutes. Remove from the heat and pass the sauce through a fine sieve into a bowl.

4. Place two peach halves in the centre of the serving plate with a large scoop of the gelato, then spoon the sauce around the peaches.

Pear and frangipane tart

Traditionally, recipes for this tart require that you poach the pears, but I have found that this method can discolour the fruit and makes the tart's base soggy after a day or so.

I use ripe, but firm pears, without poaching, and the tart is perfect every time. The pastry remains crisp, the fruit keeps its colour and the flavour is fresh.

See overleaf for the recipe

Pear and frangipane tart

Serves   8 - 10

You will need a 30cm x 4cm loose-bottomed, non-stick flan tin.

For the pastry:

220g plain flour

100g ground almonds

170g unsalted butter, softened

110g caster sugar

2 medium eggs yolks, beaten

Pinch of salt

For the frangipane:

200g ground almonds

200g caster sugar

200g unsalted butter, softened

40g plain flour

4 large eggs, beaten

50ml calvados

1½ tsp good almond extract

For the pears and glaze:

3 large ripe William pears or equivalent

75g Dr Otka's apricot glaze
(available in any major supermarket) or a lump-free apricot jam

Juice of 2 large lemon

Method:

For the pastry:

1. Grease the loose-bottomed tart tin and line the base with parchment paper.

2. Place the flour, salt and almonds on a work surface. Begin to work in the softened butter, rubbing it into the flour and nuts until a breadcrumb consistency is achieved. Make a well in the centre and add the egg yolks. Begin to draw the pastry together and press into a ball. Swiftly knead the pastry together a few times on a lightly floured surface, wrap in cling film and refrigerate for a good hour.

3. Pre-heat the oven to 180°C/Gas 4. Remove the pastry from the fridge and shape into a flat circle. Place a large piece of cling film underneath the pastry, place another piece on top and with a rolling pin begin to shape into a round, about a ¼ inch thick. It will need to be roughly 14 inches in diameter to fit the flan tin.

4. Line the flan tin with the pastry and prick it all over with a fork (including sides). Place both pieces of cling film just used on top of the pastry with a piece of parchment over the top, the cling film should go over the edges to prevent them catching (the film doesn't melt). Place baking beans into the tin and blind bake for 12 minutes, until only just beginning to brown. Remove from the oven and allow to cool.

For the frangipane:

1. Place the ground almonds, sugar and butter into a food processor bowl and pulse. Add the eggs and pulse, then add the flour and pulse, then the calvados and almond extract and run for a couple of seconds until combined. Leave the mix in the bowl.

2. To prepare the pears, first, take a large flat plate, and squeeze the juice of one large lemon over the surface. Peel the first pear and slice in half vertically. Carefully remove the core and the stem fibre. Then slice the pear's flesh horizontally in quarter-inch slices, so that you have small arches of fruit. Gently fan the arches into a cascade, then lift carefully with a palette knife, and place on the plate, squeezing a little lemon juice on top (this is to prevent the pear flesh turning brown). Repeat this process with the remaining pears.

3. Spoon the frangipane mix into the pastry case, ½ cm from the top.

4. Dust the pear halves with icing sugar (this will ensure the pears have a lovely caramelised sheen). The flan requires that you have a five-pear circle, then the sixth pear is used to fill the centre (only half will be used). Carefully lift the pears from the plate using a palette knife and lay the fruit on the frangipane mix, with the stem ends pointing to the centre. Do not press the pears down into the frangipane.

5. Cook the tart for 35 – 45 minutes. Once the frangipane is golden brown and springy to the touch, remove from oven and allow to cool.

6. Once the frangipane has reached a cool temperature, brush the surface with the apricot glaze. Do not apply the glaze when the frangipane is hot. Serve warm or cold, according to taste. I recommend vanilla ice cream as an accompaniment.

Rich orange-scented, dark chocolate fondants

A well-executed chocolate fondant never fails to impress - the key is not to overcook. There is nothing more disappointing than a dry centre. Keep an eye on them in the oven and be brave – better to be slightly under-done than dry!

Serves   6

You will need 6 x 175ml individual moulds.

Ingredients:

300g good quality dark chocolate, minimum 70% cocoa solids

100g unsalted butter, soft, plus a little for greasing

120g caster sugar

4 large eggs

1 tsp vanilla extract

50g plain flour, plus a little for dusting

Zest of 1 orange

A little cocoa powder to dust

Method:

1. Pre-heat the oven to 200°C/Gas 6. Put a baking sheet in to warm. Lightly butter the moulds and dust with flour, tapping away any excess.

2. Break up the chocolate and gently melt in a bain marie, taking care that the water doesn't touch the base of the bowl. When there are small lumps of chocolate left, remove the liquid from the heat, as the lumps will melt in the residual heat.

3. While the chocolate is cooling slightly, cream together the butter and sugar until pale and fluffy, then gradually add the eggs, one at a time (if the mix begins to curdle, simply add a pinch of flour). Add the vanilla extract, orange zest and sift in the flour. Once a smooth batter has been achieved, stir it into the chocolate and blend well.

4. Divide the mix evenly into the moulds using a spoon. Place the moulds on the pre-heated baking sheet and bake for 6−7 minutes but no more. Remove from the oven and with a cloth-wrapped hand, as they're hot, take each mould and run a knife around the fondant's edge to loosen them. Then turn them out directly onto the serving plates. Dust with cocoa powder and serve with clotted cream.

Tiramisu

Tiramisu is well loved and extensively documented. This recipe is very simple, yet the one we are most asked for. The mascarpone cream can also be used separately, spooned over marinated fruits. I've also served it as an accompaniment to summer pudding.

Serves   6 - 8

You will need a 7cm deep, 28cm x 20cm dish or baking tray.

Ingredients:

1½ bags savoiardi biscuits *(aka lady fingers)*

500g mascarpone cheese

1.25 litres double cream

500ml espresso coffee, cooled

15ml coffee essence *(such as Camp)*

6 large egg yolks

100g caster sugar

30ml sweet marsala wine

100ml Tia Maria liqueur

200ml Kahlua *(or Illyquore)*

50g cocoa powder

Method:

1. Express the coffee shots, place in a shallow bowl and allow to cool. Once cold, measure the wine and liqueur and add to the coffee.

2. Lightly whip the cream to soft peaks, cover with cling film and refrigerate until needed.

3. Gently heat the egg yolks and caster sugar in a bowl over a bain marie and whisk until the mix becomes pale, creamy and has thickened. Remove from the heat and allow to cool.

4. Once cold, begin to fold in the mascarpone cheese and whipped cream and leave to one side.

5. Dunk the savoiardi biscuits into the coffee mix for a second or so, but don't allow them to become soggy. Arrange them in rows that cover the base of the dish. To this layer add half the mascarpone mix and smooth over with a palette knife, ensuring that the mix extends right into the corners and sides. Repeat the sponge finger layering process once more and spread the final layer of mascarpone cream on top. Dust with cocoa powder and refrigerate for at least four hours before serving.

The Basics

How to prepare a bain marie

A bain marie can easily be rigged at home. All you need is a deep pan and a glass or metal bowl with a rim slightly wider than the pan's rim, and a bottom that will fit down in the pan. If the pan is too small or the bowl is too big, the heat will be concentrated right at the very bottom of the bowl. You want as much of the bowl to be inside the pan as possible to promote even heat distribution.

To use a bain marie correctly, put about 2 - 3 inches of water in the bottom pan, and put the pan on the hob on a medium heat. Then, place the bowl over the pan and add your ingredients. Make sure that the bottom of the bowl does not touch the water when it is inserted. Whisk the ingredients constantly and control the heat so that the water maintains a simmer, not a vigorous boil.

Why make fresh pasta dough?

The making of fresh pasta is a daunting prospect for most novice cooks... But, if you take your time and follow a few basic rules (and tips), you will succeed.

Why bother? Well... fresh, homemade pasta is hard to beat. To be fair, dried, shop-bought pasta is fine for many dishes, but fresh raviolis and tortellini do demand fresh pasta, so that the fillings can be introduced to produce the desired outcome.

The first time I made fresh pasta, many years ago, I endured an utterly disappointing and frustrating afternoon. However, over the years, I have learned a few tricks of the trade, and have managed to identify pitfalls and challenges that can be overcome (with practise!).

In this recipe I have introduced semolina flour, which guarantees that sought-after al dente bite. I also suggest that you make the dough by hand, so that you develop a 'feel' for the consistency of the dough. However, if you prefer, you can use a processor, although that's perhaps best left to those who have made fresh pasta by hand before and, therefore, know what to look for in it's texture.

See overleaf for the recipe

Basic pasta dough

Ingredients:

(This recipe yields approximately 1kg of pasta)

700g '00' pasta flour

100g fine semolina flour

9 medium egg yolks, plus 4 whole medium eggs, beaten

A good pinch of fine salt

Method:

1. Sift both flours and the salt together directly onto a work surface and mix well. Make a large well in the centre and pour in the beaten eggs, drawing the flour into the well. At this point the eggs will attempt to run all over the work surface, so work with some haste to draw the flour in to soak up the egg.

2. Now lightly dust the work surface with flour and begin to knead the dough. The kneading process is essential as it releases the gluten in the flour, which ultimately stabilises the dough. Knead for at least five minutes. The dough will become more elastic while you work, as a result of the gluten. When the dough has a spring-like touch, gather into a ball by tucking the dough under itself a few times to create a dome. The surface should have a soft sheen.

3. Wrap in cling film, as the dough dries quickly. Leave the pasta to rest for an hour and assemble a pasta machine.

4. When the hour is up, take a couple of damp tea towels, lay one out to the left of the pasta machine and have others at the ready. Unwrap the pasta and cut into four equal sections. Immediately re-wrap the remaining sections and set aside. Set the machine to its widest setting (usually no.1 but do check the instructions). Shape the quarter-portion into a flattish oblong with your hands, and begin to run the pasta through the machine. Support the dough as it emerges from the machine with the back of your hand. The pasta is now a long oblong shape. Place this on the prepared tea towel and fold one side to the centre of itself, then fold the other side over that. Now you have a three-layered oblong. Pass the folded edge through the machine again on the same setting. Repeat the same rolling and folding process three more times on this setting. Now turn the machine to the next, thinner setting (no. 2). Run the dough through, supporting it as it comes through the machine's rollers. You only need to run the pasta through once on each setting from now on. Place this larger sheet back onto the tea towel (otherwise the dough will stick to the work surface).

5. Cut the sheet in half and place one half on another damp tea towel and fold the towel over to prevent it from drying out. Set the machine to the next, thinner setting (no. 3) and roll the other half through in the same way as before, always supporting it as it comes through. As the sheets get longer, the dough becomes very delicate and difficult to handle, just be gentle and never stretch or pull the dough.

6. Keep repeating this process until you have reached the thinnest setting on the machine. As one half is finished, place it on a damp tea towel and cover it. The sheets will get longer and longer. The important thing is to lay the finished sheets on damp tea towels, covered, and remember which sheets have been through the entire rolling process. When you have rolled each piece through all the settings, the pasta is made. The only problem is you now have to repeat the process with the remainder of the dough!

Red wine jus

Ingredients:
(makes 1 litre)

60ml groundnut oil

4 banana shallots, finely chopped

350ml port

350ml good red wine

1 bay leaf

1 blade of mace

1.5 litres homemade veal or beef stock

3 tsp of cold butter

Sea salt and freshly ground black pepper

Method:
1. Heat a deep sauté pan on a medium heat, add the oil and sauté the shallots until caramelised. This will take around 20 – 25 minutes. They should have browned and look mushy.
2. Add the port, red wine and herbs. Bring to the boil, simmer and reduce by half.
3. When reduced, add the veal or beef stock (see page 170) and reduce by half again, to a consistency that coats the back of a spoon. Remove from the heat and push through a sieve into a saucepan.
4. Bring the jus to the boil, remove from the heat, add the butter and stir well. The jus can be used immediately, refrigerated, or frozen down.

....

Homemade mayonnaise

Ingredients:
(makes 600ml)

3 medium egg yolks

60ml white wine vinegar

500ml vegetable oil/rapeseed oil

1 tsp English mustard

Juice of ½ a lemon

Pinch of salt

Method:
1. Add the salt, mustard, half the vinegar and egg yolks to a food processor's bowl with the blade attachment fixed (or use a large mixing bowl) and whisk together for one minute, a little longer if you're mixing by hand.
2. While the processor is still running, very slowly start to drizzle the oil through the feeding funnel. If mixing by hand add the oil a little at a time.
3. When the oil has been fully incorporated, add the lemon juice and pulse again for a couple of seconds. If it becomes too thick, add a little hot water.
4. Season to taste.
5. Store in a clean jar and refrigerate.

Fresh basil pesto

Ingredients:

100g fresh basil leaves

100g pine nuts, toasted

60g Parmesan

2 cloves garlic, crushed

170ml best quality extra virgin olive oil

Juice of ½ lemon

Sea salt and freshly ground black pepper

Method:

1. Place all the ingredients, except the oil into a food processor bowl.

2. Begin to pulse the mixture and, with the motor still running, drizzle in the olive oil through the processor's funnel, until the pesto thickens.

3. Season and either use immediately, or store in a clean jar.

....

Pomodoro sauce

Ingredients:

4kg large, fresh, plum tomatoes

10 fat garlic cloves, crushed

150g fresh basil leaves, torn

1 large white onion, finely chopped

4 celery stalks, finely chopped and de-strung

175ml extra virgin olive oil

Sea salt and freshly ground black pepper

Method:

1. Make small crisscross incisions at the tomatoes' cores, place them in a large mixing bowl and pour freshly boiled water over them. Leave to stand for 10 minutes, then cut out the cores, peel away the loose outer skin and discard.

2. Heat the olive oil in a large, heavy-bottomed stockpot; add the onions and celery and sauté until translucent. Add the crushed garlic and cook for one minute.

3. Add the tomatoes, whole not chopped. Turn the mixture thoroughly so it is well combined. Reduce to the lowest possible heat on the smallest ring on the hob and put the lid on the pan. Cook down for three hours, stirring intermittently.

4. After which time, remove the lid and add 100g of the basil. Season well and stir through. Increase the heat slightly and simmer for one hour, without the lid.

5. Remove from the heat and stir in the remaining fresh basil, season and leave to cool.

6. Once cold, refrigerate in an airtight container.

Veal or beef stock

Ingredients:

(makes 1 litre)

1kg veal bones or beef marrow bones, or both

2 large carrots peeled and cut into 4 pieces

2 large onions, cut into quarters, skin on *(this adds colour to the stock)*

250ml white wine

3 celery stalks

2 garlic cloves, peeled

4 large plum tomatoes

1 sprig rosemary

4 sprigs thyme

8 whole black peppercorns

2 bay leaves

1 tsp salt

Method:

1. Set the oven to 220°C/Gas 7. Place the bones in a deep roasting tray. Put them on the top shelf of the oven and roast for 30 minutes, turning once until they begin browning at the edges.

2. Now add the carrots, onions and celery to the tray, turn the mixture around and bake for a further 15 minutes.

3. Remove the roasting tray from the oven and transfer the mixture to a large stockpot. Put the tray on the hob, on a medium heat and deglaze the pan with the white wine, scraping up all the caramelised bits and add this to the stockpot. Add all the remaining ingredients to the pot with enough water to cover everything (about 3 litres) and bring to the boil. As soon as it reaches boiling point, remove any floating scum and lower the heat. Place a lid on and leave a small steam gap. Gently simmer the stock for four hours.

4. After which time, strain the stock through a fine mesh sieve into a large bowl and allow to cool completely.

5. The stock is now ready for use, or can be refrigerated, or frozen.

Effortless chicken stock

Ingredients:

(makes 2 litres)

2 chicken carcasses, raw, with giblets *(roast the carcasses first if you require a darker stock)*

2 large carrots

1 onion, skin on

1 large leek

4 celery sticks

3 large garlic cloves

7 whole black pepper corns

10g flat leaf parsley, with stalks

3 bay leaves

2 sprigs thyme

Sea salt

Method:

1. Place all the ingredients except the salt in a large stockpot or pan with 2½ litres of water and bring to the boil.

2. Skim off any scum that comes to the surface, lower the heat and gently simmer for two hours.

3. After this time, strain, add the salt and leave to cool. Use immediately, keep refrigerated for up to two days or freeze.

Shellfish stock

You will need a muslin and some string

Ingredients:

(makes 2.5 litres)

1kg shellfish shells *(any will do, raw prawn shells, heads and tails, crab/ lobster shells etc.)*

10 scallop corals

15ml dry white wine

Skin and outer layer of 4 onions

2 celery stalks, peeled, de-strung and roughly chopped

3 leeks sliced lengthways

2 carrots, chopped

2 sprigs thyme

Several sprigs parsley

2 bay leaves

15 whole black peppercorns

2 tsp sea salt

Method:

1. Pre-heat the oven to 200°C/Gas 6. Start by bashing any large shells, such as lobster or crab, into pieces with a meat hammer, but not too small. Put the shells into the pre-heated oven and roast for around 10 minutes. Don't roast smaller, translucent shells such as shrimp or prawn shells.

2. Tip all the shells (roasted and uncooked) into a large pan/stockpot. Cover the shells with 2.5 litres of water, to 2cm above the shells. Bring this to a gentle simmer for roughly 30 minutes on a moderate heat. Do not boil the liquid; aim for a mild simmering action. The mixture will develop a bubbling foam on the surface, which must be constantly removed with a slotted spoon. Do not stir the stock at this point, as this will cause all the impurities, which would have sunk to the bottom, to rise and muddy the liquid. Gently simmer the shells for an hour.

3. When the stock has stopped foaming, tie the bay leaves, peppercorns, thyme and parsley in muslin on some string for easy removal, and add this to the pan, with the string draped over the outer rim of the pot

4. Add the wine, onions and all other ingredients, except the scallop corals. Bring to a very low simmer for about 40 minutes, skimming away any surface foam. After 40 minutes add the scallop corals and simmer for five minutes or so, add the salt and remove from the heat.

5. Press the stock through a fine mesh sieve into a large bowl. Discard the solids, and leave to cool. The stock can be used immediately, refrigerated for up to two days, or frozen down.

Index

Index

Anchovy wrapped quails eggs

See page 17 for the recipe

Inspired by what I'd learnt, I wanted to develop my understanding of the industry, so started on a two-year course in Catering and Hotel Management. At the end of this, I was proud to be able to call myself fellow of the Hotel Catering and Institutional Management Association. This led me down the road to a series of hotel general management roles with the Kingsmead Group, culminating in area management.

Of course, anyone in my profession has a dream of running and owning their own restaurant. And that I achieved by launching and running Raffles Restaurant in sleepy Aldbourne - a picturesque village on the Wiltshire downs. This rapidly became a byword for fine dining amongst the racing fraternity at Lambourne and nearby Swindon's fast-expanding business leaders, who regularly used the restaurant to entertain their clients and customers.

Further challenges followed in rapid succession. I was approached to develop a rundown gothic pile in Warwickshire, which, with the support of Michael Quinn MBE, who joined as both head chef and director and who I recruited from the Ritz Hotel in London, I built up to become the nationally acclaimed Ettington Park Hotel. Ettington won three national awards for its excellent food and luxurious accommodation for three years running during my time there.

Next came another approach - this time in Newbury - to oversee the build and develop a brand new hotel, restaurant and golfing course. This was the acclaimed Donnington Valley Hotel, which continues to attract rave reviews from the national media even today.

This was followed by another challenge, to develop a private members' dining club in Kensington, a move which happily led me to meet my wife and partner Emelia — the author of this book.

Together we opened the first Aqua on Bristol's Welshback in 1998 and a further four have now been added. We have Aqua in Bath, another Aqua in Whiteladies Road, Bristol, Aqua in Portishead and, most recently, Aqua in Milton Keynes. This continuing expansion and development of the Aqua brand now benefits from the support and help of my son Ben as operations manager of the group, and my other son Toby.

The adventure continues. We still have plans to further expand the Aqua brand, while my role with Smiths of Smithfield points to further restaurant development in the central London area. But there is always one clear goal — to deliver great value food and wines in hospitable, stylish but relaxed surroundings, and to leave customers feeling that both their time and money have been well spent!

Richard Smithson

When I walk into any of my restaurants, or the London restaurants Smiths of Smithfield and Spitalfields, of which I am chairman, I can immediately empathise with every member of the teams working there.

Why? Because whatever their role, be it the chefs and the kitchen team, the bar staff, the waiters and even those who wash up and clean — I have at some time in my long career done the same, so I understand the importance of their different roles. I understand how every one of them makes a major contribution to our customers' dining experience. Anything from a dirty glass, to poor attention to service or an imperfectly prepared meal will ruin that experience and spoil their memory of us.

Developing and building hotels and restaurants has been an exciting journey for me, and one that is far from ended. My passion and love for the restaurant business was fired by undertaking basic kitchen duties in my spare time, including washing up and basic prepping duties at the tender age of 14. From there I went on to catering college where I studied for two years intent on becoming a chef. I went on to several London restaurants where I developed my culinary skills under the tutorage of several top chefs.

You could say my love for the industry is almost an obsession, an addiction. When you feel so passionately about something it gives you the adrenaline to succeed and pass on to people what you feel so proud about. Food and drink have developed so much over the years and I feel so excited to be a part of this wonderful culture. Experiencing the vast array of different foods and wines is what I love so much, you are constantly learning all the time.

I was born into the industry! Being surrounded by food and good service in restaurants and hotels with my father. Watching and observing the hospitality industry from such a young age really gave me the confidence to do what I do today. You have to possess a keen eye for detail to deliver what guests want and expect. What I enjoyed when I was young was watching how the hotels and restaurants evolved throughout the day. It's one big living organism, they are constantly moving, living and breathing 365 days a year. You have to have eyes in the back of your head!

It was no surprise then that I wanted to join the family restaurants once I finished my studies at Christ's Hospital Horsham, and then at Cardiff University, where I read banking and finance. The restaurants were a steep learning curve from the get-go—I learnt from the bottom up. But I embraced it and took on board every experience—good and bad! During this time, I mastered my cooking skills at Bristol College through the tutoring of Theo Guy who remains a very close friend. I was then lucky enough to have the opportunity to work in London for a year at the Savoy Grill hotel—part of the Gordon Ramsay holdings. This gave me vital experience of the fine dining culture and stood me in good stead. I met my very good friend Lee Bennet who was head chef at the time. He too helped me through my early days.

I now find myself operating five restaurants with a great support network around me. I would not be where I am without my father. I am extremely proud to be working closely with him. He has guided me through my ups and downs and points me in the right direction at every turn. We have a great working relationship and seeing what he has achieved throughout his life gives me all the encouragement and motivation I need to make the restaurants a great success. Along with my father I have my loving wife Annie and son Ralph who are always extremely patient with the long hours I put into the restaurants!

Developing Aqua is now my main focus and delivering what we stand for, which is great personal service and great food that is consistent and above all exceeds our guests' expectations. This can only come to fruition through the magnificent teams in our restaurants. We have a great mix of characters, which helps us achieve our goals on a daily basis, and spending time with them makes it happen.

Ben Smithson

Acknowledgements

I would like to express my gratitude and thank certain people for their contributions towards this book.

To the chefs at Aqua, who offered their help and made themselves available to me, also for making room in the kitchens on shoot days when it wasn't always convenient! Special thanks to Paul Proudlove, who showed a keen interest at all times. To 'Chopper' (Michel Hoskins), Johny Raynard and to head chefs Joey Balcar, Liam Staddon, John Bardsley and Jamie Edwards.

To David Smithson for allowing me to use his legendary apple strudel recipe, for baking it, and for driving all the way from Oxfordshire to make it here for the shoot.

To photographers Craig Howarth and Rhys Davies who lent such an air of calmness to the proceedings - both achieved some great shots.

To Philip Pegler who very kindly stepped in to take some additional shots for the book, when I know he had more pressing things to attend to! Thank you Phil.

To Anna Smithson who gave her time to help me. Without her support and aptitude in project management the production of this book would have been a much greater challenge.

To graphic designer Sian O'Donnell, who did such a marvellous job with Anna in the visual imagery and layout.

To editors Dr Julia Hardy and Rebecca Sargent, let's face it ladies although it was a tough job, it was very, very funny at times!

Many thanks to Deborah Frewin for taking the time to test some dessert recipes; contributing to the final shoot, it was very kind of you.

I'd also like to extend my thanks to Christopher Webb for producing some last minute creative writing, we owe you lunch!

Lastly, to my long suffering husband Richard, for enabling me to write this book in the first place, without Aqua and without his love and encouragement it would never have happened. Thank you my darling x.

AQUA The Kitchen by Emelia Schiavetta

First published in 2014 by Aqua Italia Limited

153 Whiteladies Road
Bristol
BS8 4DH
UK

Tel: +44 (0) 117 973 3314

info@aqua-restaurant.com
www.aqua-restaurant.com

ISBN No: 978-0-9931021-0-3

Recipes, Text & Photographs © Emelia Schiavetta
Text Editing by Rebecca Sargent & Jules Hardy
Project Co-ordination by Anna Smithson
Designed by Sian O'Donnell
Photography by Craig Howarth, Rhys Davies & Phil Pegler
(See acknowledgments for other contributors)

Printed & bound in the UK by Taylor Brothers

Visit www.aqua-restaurant.com to read more about Aqua and the restaurants.